Halfway Thru My 20s

To Deja Wilson,
Thank you for the support!
You inspire me so much!
I hope you like the book!

Enjoy!

Halfway Thru My 20s

Stories and Lessons for Young Adults

CHRISTOPHER SUMLIN

Photo of the author courtesy of Jaylen Poland, JPVisuals LLC

Book design and production by Columbus Publishing Lab
www.ColumbusPublishingLab.com

LCCN: 2021907451

Paperback ISBN: 978-1-63337-499-7
E-book ISBN: 978-1-63337-500-0

1 3 5 7 9 10 8 6 4 2

Dedication

TO MY FATHER, ET, who has taught me so much about life through example. Dad, your ability to be warm, generous, and authentic is matchless. Each day I do my best to make you proud. Thanks for being my dad.

To my beautiful mother, Monica, who is the most supportive mother ever. Mom, I thank God for choosing you to be my mother. I appreciate you so much, and I live to make you proud. Thanks for being such a sweet soul and a fantastic mom.

To my family, friends, and loved ones. Thank you for loving me simply for who I am and for your prayers, good wishes, and positive energy. It is a great feeling to be loved and appreciated by a massive community of people who stand by and root for me. Thank you so much, because without you all, there would be no The Chris Sumlin.

CONTENTS

Dear Reader,

TODAY IS DECEMBER 26, 2019. Yesterday I spent Christmas Day in Baldwin Hills, California, with a beautiful couple, Larry and Bobbette, whom I met in 2015 when I was attending Morehouse College. Whenever I am in Los Angeles, they treat me like family, and I often spend holidays with them.

As I sat in Larry and Bobbette's living room yesterday, patiently waiting to watch some holiday basketball, the Wi-Fi stopped working, leaving me with no cell phone reception and no access to any streaming service or cable. I had been expecting to watch basketball and be on social media wishing friends Merry Christmas; instead, I found myself in deep reflection on the upcoming new year. I thought about the pacing of the past year and how I was feeling about 2019 coming to an end. Around the corner was 2020, a new start and a new year.

Christmas, New Year's Eve, and New Year's Day always fly by, and then comes my birthday. On January 7, 2020, I will have the great honor of turning twenty-six years old.

Being twenty-six is fine with me; I'm still extremely young and have so much more life to live. I feel that for many people, the twenties are a time of exploration, experimenta-

1

tion, and bad decisions. Yep, you read that right, "bad decisions." When I listen to older adults reflect on their twenties, I so often hear, "I was a wreck in my twenties," or, "The twenties were such a wild time for me." At nineteen, I had decided that I wanted to be intentional about making the best choices I could to ensure I got in as little trouble as possible. I didn't want to make hasty decisions that I would have to pay for later. Now in my mid-twenties, I'm pleased to say I'm proud of who I've become. I've made some great friends, earned three college degrees, and published two books.

As I sat there on Christmas day waiting for the Wi-Fi to return, I was struck with an epiphany. The entire idea for a book flashed into my head. The ideas came fast but were fierce. I thought about my first book, *Dealing with this Thing Called Life,* which I wrote when I was twenty-one. The goal of that book was to inspire readers of all ages. My second book, *Dealing with this Thing Called College*, I wrote when I was twenty-four. That book was written to inform young readers about the pitfalls of college life. My idea for a third book was different.

Early adulthood can be some of the most significant and vital years in anyone's life. A lot happens between eighteen and twenty-four. On that Christmas Day when the idea for this book came to me, I imagined creating a book that could inspire young adults. This wouldn't be a book for high schoolers heading off to college, or a self-help book for all ages. This book would be personal and be written for young adults looking to find their way.

Halfway Thru My 20s is a collection of personal essays, blogs, and stories all based on experiences in my life from age nineteen to age twenty-five. This book conveys how to make a real friend, how to build self-confidence, and how to avoid many mistakes that people make in their early years of adulthood. Of course, there are funny moments, lots of advice, and even a little bit of Beyoncé. I can say with confidence that this book is my best storytelling effort yet.

There is significant value in storytelling. Looking at the history of the African oral tradition, I recognize that sometimes storytelling was all Africans had. For centuries, African people relied on oral tradition to teach villagers and listeners important traditional values and morals. I know that when I hear a passionate retelling of someone's lived experience, I grow so much.

I'm grateful for the opportunity to be able to write books and share my stories with you. It is my hope that when you read my personal stories, you learn some valuable lessons and come away inspired. If you put this book down and feel just a tad bit better about early adulthood, then I've done my job. I look forward to hearing your biggest take-aways. Happy reading!

Sincerely,
Chris Sumlin

CHAPTER 1

Finding a Friend

If you go through Morehouse without finding one true,
real friend, it's safe to say you did Morehouse wrong.
                                        –Dr. Marcellus C. Barksdale

FRIENDSHIP IS FASCINATING TO ME.

It blows my mind how we as humans just select people and say, "This is my friend." I have two brothers and one sister. I grew up in Columbus, Ohio, and I considered my cousins and siblings my first best friends. We had that bond of being family. Naturally we would break bread together, have sleepovers, and create magical memories. I was comfortable with my family because I knew that by definition these individuals were supposed to have my back and care for me; they were my tribe.

I enjoyed growing up with my cousins and siblings because we had a sense of community that always felt good. I vividly remember many summer nights and weekends consisting of snacks, movies, and *Mortal Kombat* video games. However, we began to drift apart as we all became teenagers. Girlfriends and boyfriends came into the picture, extracurricular activities absorbed our time and attention, and our relationships shifted.

5

Life drastically changed for me in 2013, when at age nineteen I ventured off to college. I believe that no matter where we go, we all have an innate desire to belong, be accepted, and validated. As a kid, my family filled that void. Once I went away to college, I instinctively knew that I should have friends who would be there for me like my family, but that it would take a lot more effort to solidify those relationships.

I went to Morehouse College, an all-male, historically Black college in Atlanta, Georgia. When I was a student there, from 2013-2017, approximately twenty-three hundred students were enrolled each year. That was fine with me, because a major reason I decided to go to Morehouse was its smaller size. It was my hope that I would not only gain a fantastic education, but also be part of a thriving community where I could make lifelong friends. Morehouse prides itself on being an institution rooted in brotherhood, excellence, and service. I knew Morehouse would help me find friends I could have for life.

Having friends from different cultures and backgrounds is fantastic. But I had always envisioned myself being best friends with another Black brother that I could relate to. In the world of Trayvon Martin and the #BlackLivesMatter movement, being a Black man today is challenging. There are nuances and demands on Black men that other individuals from different backgrounds don't have to try to manage. I knew that being at Morehouse, I would find another brother to bond with—or at least I hoped I would.

At Morehouse, I quickly found mentors and guys who were like big brothers to me. These gentlemen were the ones I would call when I needed advice on classes, help navigating campus, or rides around Atlanta. These "big bros" were great, and I appreciated them, but I didn't want just that, I wanted peers.

In my pursuit of finding my tribe, I made many decisions that I thought would increase my chances of making friends. I would go to Wal-Mart and buy more snacks than I needed so if someone was hungry, I could be there to be generous. I thought, *Generosity is a sure way to make a friend, right?* More times than not, my door stayed open. I tried to play music in my room so if a brother heard a song that he liked too, maybe he would come in and talk to me and even get a pack of fruit snacks. Within my first few days of being on campus, I joined the Morehouse College Glee Club, and I sang first tenor for my entire freshman year. I hoped that maybe one or even a group of my glee club brothers would fill my need for friendship.

When I came back to Morehouse to embark on the second semester of my freshman year, I had just turned twenty and still didn't have a best friend. Even among Morehouse's all-male, Black population, I still felt like I didn't fit in. While some guys were rushing home on Sunday evenings to watch sports, I wanted to relax and watch *Keeping Up with the Kardashians*. On Thursday nights when lots of guys headed out to Thirsty Thursdays, I wanted to stay in. Oddly enough, there were even moments when guys would host study sessions that would turn into all-nighters, but I was a morning person and wasn't good at staying up at night. I felt like an oddball.

I used to fight a lot too. When I first got to Morehouse from Ohio, I remember a lot of guys bonding over putting one another down. In the dorms, it was often called "talking shit." In the Glee Club and other circles, it was called "throwing shade." It took me a while to master comebacks and wit, but after a while, I became pretty proficient. I think the part that I missed was that the throwing shade bonding was supposed to be rooted in brotherhood and love. I used to go hard and hit below the belt; there was no love in my comebacks.

In our dorm there was a brother who used to get his hair cut by another one of my classmates because he only charged $5. One day he was feeling himself, and we got into a little verbal spar. I told him, "Aye bro, shut up with those free ninety-nine haircuts. You be gettin' lookin' like a damn clown."

In retrospect, it is clear why I struggled to make friends when I got to Morehouse. I had a goal of making a real friend and trying to connect with brothers; nevertheless, I was taking pleasure in completely tearing people down in front of others because I thought it made me look cool. My actions were incongruent with my desires, so inevitably I failed.

After a while I stopped trying. There were parts of me that felt maybe I was trying too hard, that maybe my peers could feel my desperation to create a bond and that could have been holding me back. I was definitely that kid who was always trying to be the center of attention, trying way too hard to fit in, almost to the point that I was losing myself. Looking back on those times now, I see it is possible that other guys viewed me as someone who was socially awkward.

As my first year of college moved along, I knew that I needed to make a change. Slowly but surely, I started venturing away from being desperate to make friends. I discarded the premise that I had to be one way or another. The disease to please and the urge to make friends subsided. I decided I would work on being a friend to myself first and allow life to take its course. As my confidence within myself began to grow, I started to chill out. Instead of forcing my reality to be what it wasn't, I just accepted who I was and told myself that if I was going to make a friend, it would happen naturally, and if not, that's okay because on my own, I'm already enough.

Before I arrived at this new level of thinking, during my freshman year I took a Spanish class with a professor named José Larrauri. Professor Larrauri was a short, stylish man with a low tolerance for foolishness in his class. The course took place at 9:00 a.m., and we were expected to participate in each session or points were deducted from our grades. The class was small, and as the semester progressed, more and more guys dropped the course. (It turns out the last thing college students want to do at 9:00 a.m. on a Monday is learn Spanish.) I've always been great at remembering names, so by the third week, I had all my classmates' names and hometowns memorized.

One of my classmates who stuck the course out until the very end was a cool guy from Chicago. I don't use the word "cool" heedlessly. By "cool" I mean he exhibited that quality in his demeanor, conversation, and presence. I've always been more of a firecracker, the complete antithesis of cool. This gentleman was different. He showed up for class, and although rather quiet, never missed the chance to get his participation points for the day. Through class participation, I soon learned that this cool guy from Chicago was named Corbin and that he was a freshman like me. I never spoke to him, but I knew his name and hometown. Since we were both freshmen, I was certain that our paths would cross again either in a class, in the dorms, or on campus somewhere.

The freshman dorms at Morehouse are like fraternities. Each dorm has its own culture, history, and most notably its own stroll team. In African American spaces, strolling is a line dance performed by members of a cultural organization, and it usually is done at a step show or party. Each dorm's stroll team consists of eight to fifteen guys. For weeks, the various stroll teams prepare for the Freshman Hall Stroll Off. At this big event, all of the teams compete in front of the entire school to see which dorm has the best performance.

I stayed in the Dubois International House; Corbin lived in the Living Learning Center (LLC). It would have been fun for me to be on the stroll team, but unfortunately, I didn't make the cut. Week after week, the Dubois stroll team would practice and then come back to the dorm to showcase what they had learned.

One evening after stroll practice when the stroll team returned to our dorm lobby and performed what they had learned in rehearsal, I jumped in the line, jokingly hitting the moves and making everyone around laugh. Once the dorm team finished, one of my brothers said, "Chris, you should have actually been on the stroll team. You can move." He was right. Too bad. Watching our stroll team day after day, I was jealous and wished I possessed the confidence to hit those dance moves seriously in the same way they did.

I predicted that the Freshman Hall Stroll Off would be deeply competitive since each freshman dorm had practiced so diligently. Earlier in the day of the final competition, I had been in a small fight with some guys in my dorm because I had made some bad jokes about how our stroll team was going to lose that evening. When it was time for the stroll off to begin, students ran through the dorm, linking up with their friends. I didn't have anyone to go with, so I went by myself. Walking to the venue, Archer Hall Auditorium, I was not cheering for my Dubois brothers in the stroll off. I went planning to cheer for another dorm team and to laugh at my dormmates for what I suspected might be a loss for them. (No wonder I had few friends. Look at my thinking.)

During the stroll off, I watched the LLC stroll team perform. The team came out wearing all-black suits and bright silver masks. Their theme seemed to be "Stealing the Show," and it was actually quite brilliant. Midway through the performance, one of the guys did a backflip before starting another dance number. This brother did the backflip and just barely landed on his feet. That backflip caught my eye because it was different—it was memorable. As the performance continued, the performers took off their masks, and it was then that I realized that the brother who did the backflip was Corbin from Spanish class.

The entire performance by LLC was epic. The music blared, the crowd cheered, and the brothers of LLC danced as if their lives depended on it. At the conclusion of the performance, all the guys were sweating, breathing hard, but still holding their composure in their all-black suits. From the look on each member's face, it was clear that each of the guys worked so hard on that performance. It was a tremendous moment.

That day, LLC, along with backflipping Corbin, did in fact win the stroll off, and my dorm hall lost. It was an incredible experience because each stroll team did such a good job. Any of those routines, each so flawlessly executed, could be used for a music video today. I'm sure the judges had a hard time picking a winner, but congrats to LLC because they did deserve the win. They truly stole the show.

The next morning in Spanish class, I saw Corbin walk in. Class was going as usual when I instinctively felt that I should tell him how well he did in the stroll off. This instinct was fierce. When class ended, I grabbed my books and bag as I was headed out to leave. I was in a rush because I had a science class in ten minutes. As I walked out the door, I stopped, turned to him, and blurted out, "Hey man, that backflip you did at the stroll off yesterday was cool. You killed it." I took a breath, ready for him to either cuss me out, swat me away like a fly, or do whatever he was going to do. I was sure my unfamiliar smiling face and boisterous personality were not going to resonate with this brother, especially this early in the morning.

To my surprise, he looked up at me with a big smile and said, "Thanks, man. I was so nervous I almost fell, but I caught myself and had to keep going. I was just so happy we won." I congratulated him once again. I remember him going on and on about the performance and how he felt about it all. He opened up like a book, his words seeming genuine and humble. Corbin talked more than I did and almost caused me to be late for my next class. I walked to science class thinking, *That dude is cooler than I thought. I'm gonna have to talk to him more.*

We exchanged small talk at each class after that. I saw him at a party with his dorm mates once. We then shortly became Facebook friends and gradually started hanging and talking.

As life would have it, we ended up taking another Spanish class together that next semester. We both were taught by Professor Barbara Williams, the same exact class but at different times. Corbin took the class directly after I did, and because the textbook was expensive, I let him borrow mine. Most brothers at Morehouse shared books and helped each other out. The brotherhood aspect of Morehouse is the best part about the school; I've never experienced anything quite like it since.

When it came time for Corbin and me to take our Spanish final exam, we studied together. After that exam, we both passed the class with flying colors. After much conversation, studying for Spanish together, and sharing a textbook, we organically became true brother-like friends.

As freshman year was winding down, it became time to start preparing to become a sophomore. Still awkward and unsure of how I would navigate college, I thought it would be smart to ask Corbin to be my roommate the next school year since we did so well together in Spanish. Corbin agreed, and we decided to live in Kilgore Hall.

As my sophomore year began, I was more mature and ready for the challenges that were ahead. Now I no longer had the desire to prove myself to anyone. My disease to please was gone. When Corbin and I moved in together, we still didn't know each other that well. It took us some time to adjust to living together. Corbin was more social than I, and he would invite people into the room to play *NBA2k*, or brothers would come to visit him to get a haircut and study. I, on the other hand, hadn't yet quite figured out how to be super social.

Sophomore year was when I began reading very heavily. Between attending classes, being in the glee club, and enjoying leisure reading, I had no substantial social life. Here I was at this great institution surrounded by so many impressive people, and yet I had no desire to interact with any of them.

By sophomore year, there were definitely those classmates who began making a name for themselves on campus by entering pageants, running for student government positions, and getting involved in college life. In my experience, I still wasn't there yet. I don't recall having a barrage of friends other than my glee club brothers. I spoke up in class, and people knew me from that, but for the most part, I still kept to myself. I often would sit alone at dinner in the cafeteria, the place on campus where most of the bonding took place. There was nothing like breaking bread and catching up with your Morehouse brothers. However, I had little desire to sit with people. Instead of eating and talking, I thought it was best to eat and read. With a book in my right hand and my fork in my left, I maintained my own narrative that no one wanted to sit in the cafeteria with the weird kid reading a book.

One evening I was in the cafeteria doing my usual reading while eating. We had roast beef, mashed potatoes, and peas that day, a simple college campus cafeteria meal. As I sat there reading my book, brothers would walk by and speak. I would offer a modest acknowledgment like a nod of the head, but nothing too extraordinary. Not only did I choose to read, but I chose to sit far away from everyone else. Imagine a college cafeteria packed with students, a section of tables oddly unoccupied, and then me, all by myself with a book in hand. Although this may sound pitiful, the situation had become normal to me, and dare I say, peaceful.

During this particular dinner, I happened to look up and see Corbin walk into the cafeteria. He saw me, I waved and smiled, and he acknowledged me with a modest head nod and then proceeded to get in line for food. The fact that he didn't place his backpack down at my table assured me that he planned to sit elsewhere rather than with me, sitting all by myself with a book. *Dang. Even my own roommate isn't gonna sit with me*, I thought to myself.

Minutes later, I heard a plate hit the table directly across from me. I looked up. It was Corbin. "How long you been here for? I'm starving." He took his seat and joined me. Together we broke bread and had a good conversation. That dinner was a defining moment for me. It was then that I really felt like I had made a true friend, because not only did we have productive and positive moments in our dorm room, but we also had fine times publicly in the cafeteria.

It's incredibly easy to make friends when you're successful, have a lot going on, and are considered cool among your peers. Today I have more friends than I ever thought I would. I've found a new confidence within myself and consider myself to be "good in a room." Back then, as a sophomore, that wasn't my reality. I didn't have the social skills I have now. I hadn't published any books or received any accolades that made me cool. I was simply the kid who liked to read and was in the glee club.

This story can teach several lessons. I think the first and biggest is self-acceptance. When I was nineteen and a freshman, I tried to prove myself to everyone. I started fights in the dorm. I was a mess. It wasn't until I decided to be my own best friend first that I was able to calm down and accept myself for who I was. I stopped being rude to people.

How was I expected to make friends if I was disrespectful to those I encountered?

In Proverbs 18:24 the Bible states, "A man that hath friends must shew himself friendly." My mother used to say, "If you want to have a friend, you must be a friend." I believe that we are recipients of the energy that we put out. If you find yourself constantly putting others down and being unfriendly, many times that is how they will reciprocate. When you meet people with love, empathy, and compassion, more times than not, others will do the same.

It also is important to accept the truth that genuine relationships and camaraderie take time. Frequently, when I have been in a new environment, I have attempted to hotwire a connection with someone so I'm not alone. Have you ever met someone and within the formative moments of your relationship, they begin to pour out their heart and reveal their most sacred secrets? Often when individuals do this, they are trying to hotwire and establish a relationship quickly. This method rarely leads to a long-lasting connection.

Sometimes it's okay to be alone, feel people out, and move slowly. The goal should be to establish a real bond with someone over time. Good things take time. When you meet a person, just take it step-by-step. When they communicate, try to be a sincere listener with an open heart. People will show you who they are if you take the time to listen authentically. Also, do your best to communicate your desires, preferences, and opinions with others. Don't be afraid to share purposefully who you are as a person.

A successful friendship, bond, or connection requires both parties to participate. If your new friend is doing all of the talking, expressing vulnerability, and sharing but you aren't, you are doing both of you a disservice. Make it a point to actively participate in the relationships you find yourself in.

Another insight to take away from this story is how important it is to find friends who accept you for you. Back then I wasn't half the man I am today. Today I have to turn down invitations to dinners, parties, and social gatherings. I have the pleasure of an abundance of people who want to sit with me, talk with me, and be my friend. When I was a college sophomore, I didn't have any of those things. Corbin was kind enough to accept me publicly when I was at a lower point than I am now. It was one thing to be roommates and hang in the room where no one could see; it was another to sit in the front of the cafeteria with the loner who was reading a book.

If you have a person in your life who only hangs with you in secrecy but denies you in public, they are not someone you should associate yourself with. If, in that person's eyes, you aren't cool enough, cute enough, or good enough, act quickly and find better people to be around. You are enough just as you are. No one is perfect, but everyone is worthy of love and belonging no matter who they are, where they come from, or if they want to read alone in the cafeteria at dinnertime. There are enough people in the world that you can find someone to hold you down and have your back.

Authentic friendship is a magnificent experience that many people do not get to have. A OnePoll and Evite study of two thousand Americans found that a staggering "45 percent of adults find it difficult to make new friends, with 42 percent citing introversion or shyness as the reason for their struggle."

I admit that making new friends is difficult, but it is indeed worth the effort. Every man deserves homies and boys. Every woman should have girlfriends. I do not know where we as a culture have lost the desire for positive platonic relationships. Social media seems to have perpetuated this idea of not trusting people and having "frenemies," and it needs to stop. Having Corbin as a friend has been a fantastic ride. I hope that after hearing this story you too will find some good company and real friends to surround yourself with even if it takes a little time.

CHAPTER 2
Legally Lit

It's easier to prevent bad habits than to break them.
–Benjamin Franklin

TODAY I CAN CANDIDLY SHARE that I have had more drunken nights than I can count. I have been called the life of the party by friends and even have been accused of being an alcoholic by people whom I considered family. I believe that with every label, accusation, or rumor, there is always the truth and then there is the lie. I would be remiss if I did not discuss my relationship with drinking in this book. So, here is my truth.

In the spring of 2015, I was in my sophomore year at Morehouse. I was twenty-one years old. Twenty-one can be a monumental age for anyone. Twenty-one is the age one can legally adopt a child, obtain a concealed weapons permit, and most notably for me, buy alcoholic beverages.

On my twenty-first birthday I went on an amazing date with a beautiful woman named Tyler Imani whom I had met when I was eighteen years old. We worked together at the Express clothing store in Easton Town Center in

Columbus, Ohio. Tyler was a good friend and knew that I was turning twenty-one. During the first week of January we started Facebook messaging to coordinate our plans.

Adobe Gilas is a Tex-Mex restaurant that serves really good burgers, tacos, and of course, margaritas. Growing up in Columbus, Ohio, I used to go to Easton a lot as a teenager. Walking around the mall, I often wished I could go to Adobe Gilas, so when it came time to choose where to celebrate my twenty-first birthday with Tyler, I knew this was the place.

As we sat down for our dinner and the menus arrived, I didn't know what to get as my first drink. So, of course, I went with what sounded familiar and ordered a frozen strawberry margarita with a sugar rim. I recall the bartender giving me a weird look when I asked for sugar instead of salt around the rim. It was a defining moment. I felt a sense of pride that I was "grown up" enough to be out with a lovely lady and old enough to legally drink. Following my margarita, I ordered a shot of whiskey. Tequila and whiskey are quite a combination, and not one that I would recommend.

Mixing dark liquor and light liquor is never a smart move. Also, I did not make a point of drinking water after each shot. I was piling on Mexican food, tequila, and whiskey. Again, not a smart move. The evening went really well, and Tyler was great company. When I arrived back home at my mother's house later that evening, I recall barely making it up to her door. The next morning, I threw up everything I had taken in the night before. My head throbbed, my stomach turned, and the room spun. My only saving grace was holding on to the toilet for dear life. I wondered what I had gotten myself into.

"Christopher, are you okay?" my mother asked as she heard my obnoxious vomiting.

Never once did she reprimand me or make me feel bad at all. Still to this day, I'm unsure whether or not she was aware that I had been out drinking that night. Maybe she assumed I had food poisoning, I don't know. Once I finally got some water, put some food in my stomach, and recovered, I felt good. I thought that was how a twenty-first birthday should be.

As I mentioned earlier, my birthday is January 7, which was during winter recess while I was away from campus. When I returned to Morehouse for the second semester of my sophomore year, I was very excited to start buying alcohol legally. I had gone to high school for five years and had the great honor of obtaining an associate of arts degree in high school when I was just nineteen years old. Because I went to a five-year, early college high school, I was a year older than many of my classmates. The fact that I had the ability to purchase liquor and most of my classmates didn't made me special. I was able to do something coveted that others could not.

Mind you, as a sophomore, I was still going through my isolation stage. At this time, I had only a handful of good friends from both Morehouse and Spelman College. I also was in the glee club as a first tenor. If I was not in glee club rehearsal, I was in class; if I was not in class, I was in rehearsal. My second year of college became a boring routine of obligations, academics, and leisure reading. There was not much socializing going on, nor was there any desire to do so. Corbin, on the other hand, had substantial relationships around campus.

One Friday night, one of Corbin's close friends had a party to celebrate his birthday. I was tired of sitting around in the dorm watching everyone else have a fun time, so this time I decided I would go. Since I was of legal age and had cash on hand, it was my plan to buy some liquor and beer for the party. When I arrived at the apartment with bottles in hand, I was met with appreciation and excitement. There were individuals who knew my name from being in class with me but had never really seen me have fun or let loose.

It was dark, and I could see little other than figures moving about as I walked through the party. The music was the typical Atlanta hip hop. "Freak No More," "Fight Night," and "Handsome and Wealthy" by the really popular Migos were playing. Fetty Wap had a few radio singles that were popular too. In addition to hip hop music, there was smoke in the air. Looking past all the unrecognizable people packed wall-to-wall, I was able to spot a small kitchen area where I saw a sink and cups. I figured I could set up my station here. The party was lit. I felt the good vibes. As the party continued, I set up bottles and red cups and waited to see what would happen. Before I knew it, people started coming up to me.

"Yo, Bro! Weren't you in my class?" was how most of the interactions began. Someone would recognize me, initiate some small talk, and then proceed to place their cup in front of me and ask for a shot or some beer. It was a good night. I experienced a good party, made some new "friends," and got lit.

After that night, I decided to party more. Whenever there was a house party or an event around campus, it was my duty to show up with liquor. At first, all was fine. People began to learn who I was, and I was proud of myself for experiencing the stereotypical college experience. As time progressed, I learned that I could out-drink a lot of the guys on campus. I learned to eat a meal before a party and have water in between drinks so I could last longer into the night.

As time went on, drinking casually was no longer a pleasantry. It became a habit. Tuesdays meant Taco Tuesday at Prickly Pear Taqueria in Midtown. Hump Wednesdays were the AUC block party on campus where pregame drinking was essential. Thirsty Thursdays in Atlanta meant a club was hosting a party. Fridays included Market Fridays at Spelman and Happy Hour at Blu Cantina on Peters Street with margaritas and wings. Saturdays were house party nights. Sundays were for bottomless mimosas and brunch. Mondays were for recovery.

The opportunities to drink and turn up were everywhere. It was bad if you weren't turning up. You were considered cool if you could take more shots than everyone else. It was considered a good night if you forgot how you made it back home but woke up the next morning to retell your experience. Environment is everything. The fact that my environment not only presented opportunities to drink but celebrated this kind of behavior took its toll on me. My drinking became heavy. Some nights it was dark liquor, other nights light. Each turn-up night started with a Chick Fil-A sandwich and fries or a trip to the cafeteria. The more carbs I put in my system, the longer I could drink. Dark circles began to develop under my eyes. I gained a lot of weight from all the partying and lack of exercise. Eventually I had to take a trip to the campus medical center because I began struggling with hypertension.

My drinking habits were affecting not only my body but my relationships as well. My best friend Sean and I had a stern conversation about how my behavior had started rubbing people the wrong way. It was brought to my attention that there were classmates who looked at me as a bully or someone full of drama. I can always count on my friend

Sean to call me out when I get out of line, and that day he did. "Chris, are you even aware of how you act when you drink?" His question was honest and was one that I never had thought about. It took me a long time to realize what I was doing to myself, but I knew after a while that things were slipping out of my control. I look back at some of those episodes of my drunk antics and feel nothing but shame and regret.

The sad part is, while I was turning up at night, I still managed to do a lot of cool things. After my sophomore year, I landed my first television internship in Los Angeles. During my junior year, which was the year I drank the most, I also published my first book. Compartmentalization is a dangerous thing when you know how to do it well. There was one moment in time when I gave a speech on campus to inspire freshmen who had just finished their first year at Morehouse, and that very same night, I went to Moondogs in Atlanta for vodka lemonades directly following. I went from encouraging and inspiring students to do well in school to encouraging and inspiring my friends to take shots with me. I made it all look so easy in person and on social media.

When I began doing the self-work to unpack why I was binge drinking so much, I discovered how much I did not like myself. Drinking allowed me to escape and feel like Superman. The heavy drinking also made me cool and limitless. When I was intoxicated, I could say whatever I wanted, be whoever I wanted, and feel unstoppable. It was a long time before I stopped using liquor as an escape from reality and did some real soul searching. I lost many friends and hurt a lot of feelings before I finally got things under control. There are people still to this day who won't talk to me because of something I said while drunk. I still have my fun, but those heavy binge drinking nights are more random than habitual like they were in the past.

The thing about bad habits is that they don't happen overnight. First it starts with one beer, one party, and then moves to two drinks and then two parties. Then you progress to bingeing and before you know it, you've become a binge drinker.

It is important that I share my experience and express to you how vital it is to be very cautious about picking up bad habits. Drinking caused me a lot of drama and shame that could have easily been avoided. The core of my issue with drinking was to use it as an escape from reality and feel desired by those around me. Liquor should never be the medication for any of our problems. If you find yourself or someone you know getting too lit, say something. We can't continually normalize excessive drinking because society tells us it's cool or what we are supposed to do.

By no means am I advocating for abstaining from alcohol altogether. I understand the joy of a tasty lime margarita or a cool mimosa on a Sunday afternoon. I know that I am not alone in enjoying this pleasantry. According to the 2018 National Survey on Drug Use and Health (NSDUH), 86.3 percent of people ages eighteen or older reported that they drank alcohol at some point in their lifetime; 70 percent reported that they drank in the past year; 55.3 percent reported that they drank in the past month. It is clear that people drink and enjoy doing it.

My intention in sharing this story is to bring awareness to how easy it is to pick up a new bad habit and make poor choices. It is also crucial that I tell my truth to advocate for drinking responsibly. When I hear songs with lyrics such as, "Blame it on the vodka, blame it on the Henny," like "Blame It" by Jamie Foxx, or songs like "Shots" by LMFAO, I understand that there are a lot of messages in pop culture that normalize excessive drinking. When we normalize bad behavior, it costs.

An estimated eighty-eight thousand people (approximately sixty-two thousand men and twenty-six thousand women) die from alcohol-related causes annually, making alcohol the third leading preventable cause of death in the United States. We have to do better.

According to the National Institute on Alcohol Abuse and Alcoholism, an estimated 15 million people in the US have Alcohol Use Disorder. Approximately 5.8 percent or 14.4 million adults in the United States ages 18 and older had AUD in 2018. This includes 9.2 million men and 5.3 million women. Adolescents can be diagnosed with AUD as well, and in 2018, an estimated 401,000 adolescents ages 12–17 had AUD.

Whether you are reading this book at twenty and on the cusp of the legal drinking age, or at fifty and know someone who drinks too much, we have to show people there is a better way to have fun more responsibly. We can't be complicit in bad behavior or egg it on. I cannot count the instances where someone would look at me, smile, and say, "Look at Chris. He is so lit!"

The people who expressed that sentiment were complicit and encouraged my bad behavior. Everyone wants to feel good about themselves and validated—that is part of our shared human experience. The fact that I was celebrated for my binge drinking heavily influenced me to do it more. Every morning I was hungover and laughed about how I got drunk. Every time I was told how cool I was for my drinking and was expected to be the life of the party at functions, those statements encouraged my poor behavior.

If you do find yourself overindulging in alcohol, ask yourself why. I encourage you to take the time to assess your internal or external motivation for getting drunk. For me, I had a desire to be perceived as cool and resourceful. I also struggled with self-acceptance and tried to use liquor as a Band-Aid to cover my pain. If you have some unresolved issue inside, drinking will only exacerbate the issue and cause you more harm. There is nothing wrong with getting real professional help or counsel instead of drinking to mask the pain. I can say from experience that drinking to have fun is acceptable; continual binge drinking to get drunk is not.

Environment is another major factor when it comes to drinking. We have to be mindful of the people we surround ourselves with and how those people impact our habits. My environment at the time celebrated my bad behavior and downright encouraged it. I should have been more responsible and taken care of myself by not participating in as many parties as I did. All of that time, effort, energy, and money that I used to binge drink could have led to something more productive. Environment is everything, and if you find yourself being encouraged to do something negative because of your environment, make a change quickly.

Drinking can be fun and has its place, but more times than not I see people making careless drunken mistakes that need to be addressed. We cannot normalize and encourage toxic behavior such as binge drinking. Have fun and be adventurous, but make sure you are being completely responsible whenever you are presented with an opportunity to be legally lit.

CHAPTER 3
Building a Church and Being Like Beyoncé

*If you can tune into your purpose and really align with it,
setting goals so that your vision is an expression of that
purpose, then life flows much more easily.*

–Jack Canfeld

CHURCH IS SUCH a crucial part of my identity. All I did as a kid was go to church. I never got to go trick-or-treating, I never hosted any traditional birthday parties, and I was severely discouraged from listening to secular music. My sheltered upbringing was laid out for me before I was even born, because it started with my mom and dad and the values they upheld. My parents got married in 1991. My dad was nineteen and my mother was twenty. Two years into their marriage they began having children. Dad always jokes that the reason they had so many children was because in the Pentecostal church they attended, contraceptives were not allowed.

In 1993, my older brother Orlando came into the world. He was the apple of my father's eye. They named him Orlando Cepada Sumlin, Jr. after my father. A year later I arrived and then my younger brother, William. By 1995, my parents were four years into their new marriage with three young baby boys. Mom went to college for a year at Ohio University and never finished. Dad dropped out of high school in the ninth grade to support his ill grandmother. He earned his GED years later. After they got married, Dad worked odd jobs to keep food on the table while Mom stayed at home with the babies. Times were tough, but somehow my parents always persevered, believing they were laying the foundation for something greater.

In 1995, my father worked at a United Dairy Farmers convenience store in Dayton, Ohio. During a shift at work, my father had an epiphany that he was going to start his own church. He quickly ran home to tell my mom of his plan. "The spirit of the Lord spoke to me clear as day and told me that I was gonna start a church called 'The Upper Room Deliverance Ministries,'" my dad said.

At the time, my parents were very devout Pentecostal Christians. It was a normal occurrence for them to go to church and witness church members speaking in tongues, ministers hearing from God, and the Holy Spirit moving. My mom quickly jumped on board. She believed in my father, she believed in the ability of Christians to hear from the Lord, and she believed that starting a church was for the best. With three new baby boys, no formal business training, and limited resources, my parents set out to start the church of my father's dreams. Quickly my father was able to get his state paperwork, muster up a few instruments, and begin laying the groundwork for what would be the church.

In 1996, Dad told my mother that he heard from the Lord again and felt instructed to relocate the family to Georgia. I don't know how a newlywed couple in their twenties with three new babies felt comfortable transitioning from Ohio to Georgia, but somehow they did. When my dad has a vision, he will do whatever it takes to bring that vision to life, regardless of the sacrifices. Mom was a traditional wife who loved and believed in her husband. She wasn't concerned with buying a new home or living lavishly; she was focused on investing in her husband and his vision and building a nice family.

Relocating to Rome, Georgia, was quite a trip. To my knowledge, there were no massive savings, booked flights, or even real plans—just a vision. As Mom and Dad went to start the church with their three young boys, my mother got pregnant for the fourth time.

In 1996, my parents welcomed a baby girl. Britney Nichole was born on January 23, 1996, in Rome, Georgia. My family's time in Rome was short-lived, but it exposed my parents to new people and new ideas. Years later, Dad told me that when we all lived in Georgia, he dreamed of going to Morehouse College to study. Unfortunately, with his new church and new family, enrolling in school was not a viable option.

A year later, another big transition occurred—my maternal grandfather landed a new job in Columbus, Ohio. To help my mother get more support with her new babies, my father moved us all into my grandparents' house in Columbus. I was still very young and don't recall much about that short time, but I do remember I enjoyed being with my grandparents. What I also remember is that in 1998 Dad was finally able to secure his first storefront church building to host services. With his vision in mind and no other option, Dad moved us all from my grandparents' house into the basement of the church building.

Imagine a local storefront building in a rough neighborhood. The building was no bigger than an average corner store. The windowless basement contained a small kitchen and a storage closet large enough for a full-size bed. My three siblings, my two parents, and I all lived in this basement. As bizarre as this sounds, I remember as a young child celebrating the fact that my family was moving into the church basement because I didn't know anything better. I was proud that my dad's church was coming to life right before my eyes.

The basement was our home; the upstairs was used as the church sanctuary. The storefront building had enough space for about fifty chairs, an elevated platform that became the pulpit, and a section for instruments. Dad was musically gifted and had the ability not only to preach, but also to play the keyboard and sing. Orlando kept banging on pots and pans as a child, so naturally he was the drummer. My mother was the emcee of the services and helped lead praise and worship. My brother William and I were the ushers. I remember that Britney was too young to participate, so she just clung to my mom's side with a doll in her hand while my parents sang during service. Together my family took everything we had to make sure that the church was our top priority.

In these early years, the ministry never really took off. Starting a church is just like starting a business. My dad was the founder and carried the vision, and we all supported him in any way we could. My parents poured everything they had into The Upper Room. The building was in the Linden area, on Cleveland Avenue in Columbus. Linden was a predominantly Black neighborhood where most families lived at or below the poverty line. My young siblings and I slept on mattresses on the floor in the basement. There were roaches and rats, and the storefront building lacked the essentials of a "normal" American home. I remember there was not much in our church basement home. We had no backyard to play in, no shower or bathtub, and of course no real bedrooms with Scooby-Doo stickers on the walls.

Our lives were the church and nothing more. On one hand, it was embarrassing, sad, and almost inhumane to raise small children in this environment. On the other hand, the church basement was all I knew. All I knew were church services, Bible studies, and revivals. I was expected to read the New Kings James Bible at age five. I was taught by example the importance of hard work, sacrifice, and believing in a vision. This foundation taught me some of the most powerful lessons that I still reflect on today and shaped the trajectory of my life.

As I entered kindergarten, my reading level was far beyond that of my peers because I was already used to reading and doing so aloud. There were times in Sunday school services when I read the Old Testament in front of our small congregation. I believe it was the church that caused my family and me to live a life of discipline. Church services always started on time, and there was an agenda that was followed. School was no different to me. I had learned from church how to work hard, show up on time, and behave well. I remember being the only kindergartner to get perfect attendance in my entire elementary school in 1999. I still have the trophy. Being raised in the church shaped who I was. In retrospect, I can say that my parents' zeal and their forcing us into church so much was not the stereotypical upbringing, but I wouldn't trade that experience for anything. The church taught me values and discipline and taught me how to look for the good in every situation.

In addition to being sheltered in a church, we lived in poverty. Most of the time there was one television in the household, which my father monopolized. While some children may have been able to watch Disney movies and familiarize themselves with sports teams and cartoons, I remember watching *Bobby Jones Gospel* and the Trinity Broadcast Network. By the age of seven, I could tell you every book of the Bible in order but couldn't name five sports teams. I knew traditional gospel hymns but was never exposed to Biggie or Tupac. If we were watching television as a family, it was a show my father enjoyed or a sermon by Bishop TD Jakes. Going to school, I was so ashamed to be dropped off in the morning because my dad would be blasting Bishop Ronald E. Brown or Dorothy Norwood on the car radio. I wanted to be like the other kids whose parents were pulling up to the school listening to the local hip-hop radio station. All we listened to was Joy 106.3, the local Columbus gospel radio station.

One evening Dad and I were heading to a Giant Eagle grocery store to prepare for dinner. At the time we had an older car, and when we got in it, the car radio was playing the local pop station. The song that I heard was new to me. The beat felt different; the lyrics were not over sung or reminiscent of church. When I heard this pop song, it was refreshing, different, and intriguing. It was the first time in my life I had ever heard a secular song. The radio host said that the song was "Bills, Bills, Bills" by Destiny's Child. That moment was the first time I ever heard Beyoncé's voice. It was as if a small little light came on in my head. I knew that this culture was different and that I yearned for more.

One evening in 2001, I sat with my family and watched the Michael Jackson 30th Anniversary Special. My grandfather was a radio DJ. I recall spending nights at his house and hearing of Michael Jackson, but his 30th Anniversary special really showed me who he was and his impact on pop culture. Throughout the presentation I was able to see a variety of different artists all celebrate Michael Jackson.

During the program, I heard the announcer say, "Please welcome the hottest trio in pop music today—Beyoncé, Kelly and Michelle, the Bootylicious, Destiny's Child." When the lights flashed on and the performance began, I saw Beyoncé for the first time. I had never seen a woman look like, sing like, or dance like that before in my entire life. The performance was electrifying. It was sultry, sexy, but still classy. I enjoyed seeing Destiny's Child dance in unison and get the crowd hyped. I particularly remember Beyoncé as she sang her verse. I was deeply impressed. I knew that whatever she was doing I wanted to follow and support. It was then that my love for Beyoncé began, because she was my first real taste of music that was something other than gospel music.

As I grew through my childhood and teenage years, I became familiar with other artists. Getting ready for school started with music videos, and on the school bus we listened to the local hip-hop station. I began to learn about 50 Cent, Nelly, Ashanti, and so many others. Throughout my years of middle and high school, somehow Beyoncé always managed to be at the top of the charts.

I was nine years old when Beyoncé went solo and dropped "Crazy in Love." I remember being in middle school when Beyoncé released her sophomore album, *B'Day*. When I was in high school, "Single Ladies" won Song of the Year at the Grammys. I was obsessed. I kept up with every album, performance, and interview. Aside from Beyoncé being beautiful and talented, I admired how hard she worked. Studying her career, it became clear to me that the secret to her longevity was her incredible work ethic.

I was able to witness this work ethic first-hand when I attended the Formation World Tour back in 2016 when I was twenty-two years old. The day was June 7, 2016, and I was living in New York City to start an internship for the summer. This summer I had the honor of being an intern for *The Tonight Show Starring Jimmy Fallon*. My morning consisted of an orientation at NYU, which was great. NBC did a terrific job of making sure that I had all the information I needed before I started day one of my internship. I walked out of orientation fully prepared for what I knew would be a phenomenal summer.

Following orientation, I was told to go to *The Tonight Show* at 30 Rockefeller Plaza to meet my supervisor who was another two miles away. I was exhausted, but nonetheless, I walked to Rockefeller Center in the heat of the afternoon. When I arrived at "30 Rock" to meet with my boss at *The Tonight Show*, I got a text message from my friend Kevin. Kevin is a friend I have known since I was 12 years old; he's like family to me. He is funny and loves pop culture. Earlier in the year, Kevin had bought a concert ticket to the Formation World Tour that was in New Jersey that night at the Citi Field Arena. It was his plan to be in New York to see the show, but things didn't work out. Like a good friend, he sent me the ticket with text messages that read, "Get your life from Beyoncé for me. You better live it up for the both of us. I want to live through your experience. Don't let me down."

After walking over four miles in one day, going to two different orientations, and still being jet-lagged from my flight from Atlanta to NYC, I was on my last strand of energy. I was tired, but I wasn't so tired that I couldn't teach myself how to use the subway. I pulled out my iPhone with Google Maps and quickly learned how to get from my Manhattan apartment to the Citi Field Arena where the show was taking place.

Upon boarding the train, I noticed there were hardly any seats available. I wondered where all these people could be going. Stop after stop, the train remained congested and uncomfortable. With each turn and bump, I found myself knocking into the person next to me. I got a tad annoyed from having to sit tightly between two people for that long of a time. After many stops and much patience, I finally arrived at the Citi Field stop. It looked gigantic from the train, and my heart began beating with excitement. When the train stopped, a circus hit. Every single person on the train got off at the Citi Field stop. It had to be at least a couple hundred people running off the train. At that moment, I knew all of us were on the train for the same reason—to see Beyoncé.

As I walked toward the stadium, people were running past me, screaming. You could just feel the energy from all of the fans. Everyone was so hyped and pumped. I completely forgot about the day that I had and how tired I was. Before I could even gather what was going on, I was in a Beyoncé Formation World Tour T-shirt and in my seat ready to enjoy the show.

The show was truly spectacular! Kevin is a concert junkie, so naturally the ticket he gave me was for a floor seat. It was my second time seeing the concert, but this experience was better than my first. Citi Field Arena is a baseball stadium and has no roof. Witnessing the show at the stadium on a cool New York evening made the show even cooler. Beyoncé got the crowd hyped as she began the concert with her hit song "Formation." When she was on that stage performing and dancing, everyone had smiles from ear to ear and bopped along like children. It was truly a phenomenal experience. Midway through the show, Beyoncé performed another song and stopped to gather herself. She took a sip of water, wiped the sweat from her brow, and said, "If a country girl like me can do this, you can too. I'm no different from y'all. Dream big, and it could be you on this stage."

When Beyoncé said that, I looked around at the thousands of people who filled the arena all to see one woman, one show, and to experience one moment. I thought about my journey to the concert and how much it took for me to get there. I thought about how I was just one person of the thousands who went through a lot to get to the Citi Field Arena; I wondered what everyone else's story was. How much did everyone spend on their tickets? What did it take for each and every one of those people in the stands to get to the concert? The idea of celebrity and how people spend their time, energy, and money for a concert really sat with me.

By this time, Beyoncé had already moved on to the next song and everyone around me was dancing and singing, but I began to reflect. I thought to myself, *What could I do to captivate this many people? If Beyoncé can do it, maybe I can too, whether I'm a public speaker, an author, a TV producer, or maybe even a singer.* I wondered if one day I could captivate thousands of people through my own work.

I truly believe that every human being is the same in that we all have a purpose and God-given talents. I think that Beyoncé is a person who has found her God-given talent and is using it to inspire the world. She is truly living the purpose-driven life. So often when I meet people, they have no idea what they are passionate about or what their purpose is. How many people do you know who work an odd job they hate, went to college to study a major they don't even care about, or maybe even are not doing anything at all?

For me, I love storytelling. All of the work that I do, whether it be public speaking, writing, or podcasting, is rooted in storytelling. Nothing gets me more excited than the ability to share a heartfelt story with a person or an audience. Every time I publish a blog, upload a podcast, or get in front of a crowd, I get that bubble of excitement thinking about who will hear my story and be inspired by it. Nothing feels more purposeful than sharing my story to inspire others. I firmly believe that it is what I was born to do, and it makes me come alive.

If you are a person who knows what it is that makes you come alive, congrats, because that's the first step to living a fulfilled life. Conversely, if you aren't aware of your purpose and the greatness that lives inside of you, your number one priority should be finding that out.

The National Institute of Mental Health (NIMH) estimates that 16.2 million U.S. adults had at least one major depressive episode in 2016. This represents 6.7 percent of the U.S. adult population. It has also been reported that depression is most common in ages eighteen to twenty-five (10.9 percent). Award-winning therapist and writer Dr. Barton Goldsmith is an emotional fitness expert. Dr. Goldsmith teaches that having a purpose is paramount to beating depression. He states, "I believe that if you find your purpose and share it with the world, you will be happier. This is because you are doing what is right for you, what speaks your values, and is important to your life."

I can't stress enough how each and every one of us is here for a purpose. I can say from experience that once you get in tune to what it is you are here to do, nothing will be able to stop you. There is a peace that comes with living a purpose-driven life. When you know exactly who you are and what you are here to do, your entire life changes for the better. Everything you begin to do is rooted in intention. Your time will be well spent, and you will start to attract people in your life who are purpose-driven too. Living on purpose is attractive and convicting.

One practical way to begin finding your purpose is to first come to the awareness that you have one. I've met people who don't even have language for the idea of living with purpose. Your first core belief should be that you are here for a reason. An affirmation you can begin to say in the mirror is, "I am here for a purpose." Our thoughts and words have power. By merely saying that affirmation to yourself repeatedly, your mind will alter, and you will start to believe it.

Once you believe that you have a purpose, you can start looking for what it is. I encourage you to look back at your childhood. American inspirational speaker, author, and New Thought spiritual teacher Iyanla Vanzant often says, "If you ever want to look at how something is going to end, look at how it started." Think back to your childhood before you were told you couldn't be or do something. What did you really enjoy doing as a child when no one was looking? As an adult, what do you find yourself thinking about when you are alone? Is it starting a business? Becoming a teacher? Starting a church? We live in a world where anything is possible. There are people who get paid to play video games and livestream it on YouTube. Whatever it is that you want to do is possible, and don't allow anyone to convince you otherwise.

Once you have found your purpose, next up is working at it. The only place where success comes before work is in the dictionary. Just because you know what it is that you feel you are born to do, doesn't mean you will experience success quickly or that it will come easily. You will have ups and downs and failures, but you will get better with time. While you are waiting for success, do your best to do so with a positive attitude. I believe this is why my family and I were able to live in the basement of the church and not be traumatized by that experience. My dad had the vision to create his church. After he had that goal, he didn't become Bishop Jakes the day after. A lot of hard work and sacrifices came, but we as a family endured the basement of the church with gratitude until things got better. Do your best to be as patient and kind to yourself as possible. Don't beat yourself up for any mishaps or falls you may experience. That is all a part of your journey.

As you start believing in yourself and working hard, understand that there may be criticizers and haters. Don't take it personally, because that is something that just comes with success. My father used to say, "You will always have haters, but never forget that you will also have fans."

We should aim to be like Beyoncé—find our purpose and get about the business of living it. In a promotional interview for her album *4*, Beyoncé was asked the secret to her success. She said, "I know that for me to know exactly what I was born to do at such a young age is why I've been able to do what I do as well as I do it."

At a young age Beyoncé found her purpose and kept working at becoming great. It's clear that her hard work has paid off. As of 2020, Beyoncé has won twenty-four Grammys. That's as many Grammy wins as Whitney Houston, Michael Jackson, and Mariah Carey combined. It is hard for anyone to deny Beyoncé's success. She is just one of the many successful people who have followed this formula of living on purpose, working hard, and being patient. My prayer is that after reading this story you will do the same. If you can find your purpose and follow this formula, it could very well be you packing out the Citi Field stadium or experiencing massive success one day.

CHAPTER 4

The Oprah Tweet That Shook My Campus

Remember that it is quicker to destroy than build, so be careful of what you do even with your own tongue.

–Gift Gugu Mona

PRIVACY AND DISCRETION are two things that are very important to me. As a writer, I do my very best to share the interesting parts of my journey to create inspiring content. Between YouTube videos, books, and blogs, I put a lot out into the world. I've shared stories about my financial struggles, intimate details about my friends, and even truths about times when I am battling depression. It is incredibly important to me to always be truthful, heartfelt, and generous about the stories I share. At the same time, it is also vital that I am always fair to myself by keeping some personal details private. I have to be mindful that anything I put out in the world has the potential to have a massive impact on myself and others.

Most of my readers are young adults and high school students. As such, there are certain mature topics I will never publicly write about or discuss. Out of respect for certain individuals and their privacy, I will never talk about some things publicly, and I feel that is okay.

In the world of social media, discretion has lost its place. There are YouTubers who discuss the intimate details of their relationships as a means to get subscribers to their channels. It's shocking to me when I see YouTube couples sit on camera and share their sex lives, their disagreements, or their struggles in such an open way. I've seen it all, from credit scores to bank account balances to health scares, all of which I feel are a bit too personal to be all over social media.

One of my Facebook friends once livestreamed their deceased grandmother being carried out of her home. I couldn't help but think how intrusive it felt to merely watch the livestream. It was almost as if I were a fly on the wall for a very private family moment. The woman was dead, mouth open, being carried out on a stretcher while surrounded by her family. Who was I to be a witness to such a private moment? That woman didn't know me from Adam, and here I was watching her dead departure from her home.

Here are some questions that I ask myself daily: Where do we draw the line? How much is too much? What is considered oversharing? How do we participate in social media while continuing to be respectful to ourselves and our private lives?

My mother once told me an insightful story that taught me the importance of privacy. My maternal grandmother doesn't drive. Every other weekend, my mother takes my grandmother around town to do her grocery shopping and run errands. It's a regular occurrence to call my mom on a weekend and hear her say, "Hi, Christopher. I've got you on speakerphone. I'm with Nanny."

Then my grandmother says, "Hi, Mr. Christopher. How are you, sweetie?"

One weekend, Mom and Nanny were out doing their ritual errand runs when Nanny decided to buy a particular wine for my mother to keep in her house. When they got to the grocery store, Nanny did her shopping, headed to the checkout line, and paid for her groceries. The wine bottle had been purchased and was mixed in with Nanny's groceries. As the grocery store clerk began bagging Nanny's groceries and grabbed the bottle to place it in a bag, Mom said, "Oh, don't worry about bagging that up. It's mine. I can just carry it."

The grocery store clerk did as he was told and left the wine bottle unbagged and proceeded to ring in all of the rest of the groceries. When my Mom arrived at Nanny's house, together the two of them unloaded. Once everything was finally unpacked, Nanny grabbed one of her leftover grocery bags and gave it to Mom.

"What is this for, Mama? I got everything I need," Mom said.

"This is for that wine bottle," Nanny replied.

"Oh, it's fine. I can just run it into the house. I don't need a bag."

Then Nanny explained that when she was a young girl, her grandmother always believed in using paper bags to conceal what goes into a house. Nanny said that going to the grocery store for your parents was something that was common around the neighborhood. There were always children around who would go to the local market and come back swinging bread around their heads. Nanny often said she would see milk being thrown between siblings. Nanny was not allowed to walk home from the grocery store without a paper bag to conceal whatever it was that she had just purchased. As a young girl, my grandmother always carried her items home in a paper bag, never disobeying her grandmother's orders. Nanny's grandmother had explained to her that not everyone needs to know what goes into your house. Nanny expressed that some things should just be left unknown to everyone in your neighborhood or on your block. My mother agreed with Nanny's advice and put the wine bottle in a paper bag.

That Monday my mother and I talked about how her weekend was, and I discussed with her how I wanted to share some personal thoughts I was having on my blog. I planned to share some financial troubles I was having and how it was affecting me at work. She recounted the story and told me that not everyone needs to know my every thought, just like Nanny's grandmother felt that not everyone needed to know what she was bringing home from the grocery store. "Some things are just sacred and don't belong on the internet." Just as Mom did with Nanny, I did with her, and I decided not to publish the blog.

So often we discard and discredit the sage wisdom from our elders. In the world of social media and oversharing, we sometimes share too much. We can bring so many problems on ourselves by putting so much out into the world. How often have you read a headline about a teacher losing their job because they shared on Facebook a private photo that violated school policies? Every other week I find myself reading about an individual who lost their job because of a careless mistake that involved the internet.

On November 11, 2020, Jeffrey Toobin, 60, who was a staff writer at *The New Yorker*, was fired after senior colleagues saw Mr. Toobin masturbating while apparently on a separate video call. After twenty-seven years of work, Toobin was fired, disgraced, and a national headline for a careless mistake. When we aren't mindful of what we share online, we can cause ourselves a world of problems.

Today as I write this book, I think I have finally grasped the lesson of being mindful of what I share online. I deeply understand the importance of being respectful to myself and others when posting. In retrospect, this lesson would have been incredibly helpful to have learned back in 2016 when I wrote one tweet that shook my college campus.

For as long as I can remember, I have always been a fan of the Oprah Winfrey Network (OWN)—from *Iyanla Fix My Life* to *Super Soul Sunday*. I started watching OWN while I was in high school and living with my parents in Columbus, Ohio. It became a family ritual to sit together and watch Tyler Perry's *The Have and the Have Nots*. Those nights are some of my most precious memories with my parents and siblings. My support for OWN continued to grow into my college years at Morehouse. The only issue was that I didn't have premium cable in my dorm room to watch OWN programming—a fact that I would later regret sharing.

It was a cool fall night on campus, and senior year had just begun. I was with my good friend Ryan George, and we were hanging out in his suite, cracking jokes as we always did. I had known Ryan for a long time. He was one of the most influential people in my Morehouse journey.

While I was with Ryan, my phone went off. It was a tweet from Oprah Winfrey reminding all her followers that a new episode of *Queen Sugar* was coming on that night. This notification was a typical one. I was and still am subscribed to Oprah's tweets. Every time she sends out a Twitter post, I get a notification on my phone. Sometimes I chime in; other times I don't. At this particular moment, I wanted to tweet with Oprah. *Queen Sugar* was a critical hit, and I was aware that Oprah would live tweet with fans during episode premieres. I wanted to be part of the conversation. What person wouldn't want to live tweet Oprah Winfrey and potentially get a Twitter mention from the billionaire mogul herself?

Without taking a breath or a moment to think, I instantly replied to Oprah's tweet about *Queen Sugar* and said, "Oprah, can I have your OWNTV app login? I wanna watch too! We don't get OWN here at Morehouse."

Looking back, I was out of line for asking Oprah for her username and password to the OWNTV app on the internet. I was also wrong for mentioning Morehouse in my tweet. To provide context, Oprah has been the most generous of donors to Morehouse and has given millions of dollars. The fact that I was letting her know that my school didn't have her network in our dorm rooms was not a smart decision.

Never once did I consider how my words or actions could affect anything or anyone. My intention was to simply get Oprah's attention and to see if she would respond to me. I have tweeted Oprah dozens of times before asking her for tuition money, free books, and advice. One time she was tweeting about the NBA Finals game, and she happened to mention me in one of her tweets, which was really cool. But honestly, more times than not, Oprah ignores my tweets. I assume it is because she does not see them. In my mind, I felt like this time would be no different.

After sending the tweet, I put my phone down and continued chatting with Ryan; then I got a notification on my phone that Oprah had replied. Unlocking my iPhone as fast as I could, I read a tweet from Lady O herself that stated, "Shame Morehouse! No OWN TV after all the Morehouse men I've supported."

My tweet was sent at 7:03 p.m. that night, and Oprah's response was sent at 7:04 p.m. She replied, quickly, and she shamed my school in the process. I was overwhelmed with thoughts, feelings, and emotions when I saw this tweet. Part of me felt proud of myself that I was able to get Oprah's attention, if even for just one minute. Another part of me was nervous that her sentiment would cause Morehouse harm. What if someone took her tweet literally and stopped donating to the school? What if she decided not to support our school? What if enrollment dropped? What if alumni were mad at me for throwing our school under the bus and then I got harmed? All of these questions flashed through my mind, and I didn't know what to do.

Ryan was pissed. "Chris, you can't do that! Oprah is our most generous donor. If you mess up our relationship with Oprah, you could ruin EVERYTHING!"

Whereas I was just a student at Morehouse and didn't really have any campus clout, Ryan was much different. He bled Morehouse through and through. He had become a role model on campus. Ryan was a student ambassador and most notably the vice-president of the student body. He wholeheartedly understood the enormity of this situation and the impact that my tweet could have on our beloved institution.

Never once did Ryan think that my behavior was cute, cool, or funny. Like a good friend, he did his best to bring me to my senses and explain just how bad this could be. At that moment, any pride that I had about getting Oprah's attention quickly changed to fear. Somehow, I felt that I could have just destroyed an entire relationship between a billionaire donor and our school because of one reckless tweet.

That night I got an email from the president's office demanding that I meet with the communications team at Morehouse. I didn't know what they were going to do to me, but I was certainly nervous.

The next day walking around campus, I felt that everyone was talking about me. Some brothers were proud and thought it was "iconic" that I was able to make such a splash on campus, while other brothers were disappointed in me that I could be so reckless. I vividly remember going into the cafeteria for lunch and having random people whom I didn't even know come up to me to express their views:

"We actually do get OWN. It's available for an upcharge in all dorms."

"I hope they take all your money off your student account since you wanna throw us under the bus."

"Wow, man. You the GOAT. One tweet has got this entire campus talking. You're a legend."

Luckily, the staff at Morehouse were extremely compassionate and kind to me. The director of communications had a heartfelt conversation with me about the importance of being mindful of what we say and how our words have power. We ended the entire meeting by her informing me that the Oprah Winfrey Network was in fact available on campus for an upcharge and that I should have considered that fact before I went tweeting my plea to Oprah. Since then, Oprah has returned to Morehouse, given $13 million, and to my knowledge has no recollection of this incident.

This entire fiasco is a perfect example of how oversharing and reckless posts can cause harm and problems. Social media has become an entire industry. According to a Pew Research survey conducted in early 2019, around seven out of ten U.S. adults (69 percent) use Facebook. That's unchanged since April 2016, but up from 54 percent of adults in August 2012. I do think it is quite difficult to participate in the world without having some type of social media presence, but if we're going to be on these sites, we have to be careful.

My intention in sharing this story with you is to remind you to be mindful at all times of everything you post. First, it is not everyone's business to know everything about you, how you feel, and what you are going through. Second, one simple post, tweet, or photo could cause you a truckload of problems that you could have avoided. I love social media, and I do think that when used appropriately it can be a powerful tool for creating opportunities. However, each one of us has a responsibility to be fair to ourselves and be mindful of what we are putting out into the world when using any type of social media platform.

Now, before I post anything, I always wonder what my post, blog, or tweet could do if it went viral. If my grandmother were to see that video or post, would she be proud? So much prayer and intention go into everything I post, even my highlights from going out to the club. I encourage anyone reading this story to be more cognizant of what they post every time.

It is also important that we do not get so caught up in clout-chasing and external validation that we dishonor others in the process. Think about mothers who discipline their children and post it on Facebook for the world to see. Nothing breaks my heart more than to see the shameful face of a child and an annoying parent narrating the fiasco and only amplifying the situation. We all have to do better.

People must also know that just because someone doesn't engage with what you are posting doesn't mean that they don't see it. There will be people who may follow you on Twitter who never like, retweet, or reply to a tweet but read everything you post. I have so many friends on Facebook whom I haven't talked to in years whose posts I see daily, and each one helps perpetuate a narrative I have about them in my mind. Lack of engagement does not equal a lack of an opinion or impact.

My hope is that after reading this story you take a step back, breathe, and think before you post anything, understanding that first, everything doesn't need to be shared, and second, your posts can have a powerful impact on more people than just yourself. Be careful.

CHAPTER 5
The Joy of Not Knowing What's Next

If you really wanna fly, learn to befriend the winds.
—Curtis Tyrone Jones

GOING TO MOREHOUSE COLLEGE was a fantastic experience. I started college at age nineteen in 2013. The person I was freshman year compared with the person I had become by graduation at age twenty-three were two totally different people. When I arrived at Morehouse, I came in planning to major in business, wore a box haircut, and didn't have a clue who I was. By senior year, I had made a core group of friends, experienced some professional success, and knew a lot more about myself. During these times I was the big brother to students similar to how upperclassmen were big brothers to me in my freshman year. I thought I had seen it all, done it all, and maybe even knew it all. But there was one thing that I didn't know during my last year at Morehouse, and that was what I would do after I graduated.

Some students go into college completely aware of their major and the career they desire and have a solid, concrete path. I remember a gentleman in my freshman dorm who knew by the second day of classes that he wanted to be a doctor. He majored in biology all the way through our four years at Morehouse and is currently in medical school. This brother had a plan, and I'm certain will be a doctor here soon. I, on the other hand, was incredibly unsure of what I wanted as a career.

In high school I used to build websites for churches and other small businesses. That hobby started when I taught myself web design and built a website for my father's church. At just fourteen, I was recording the church services, editing the videos, and selling DVDs on our church's website which I built. I wasn't sure of exactly what I wanted to do with my life, but I knew that I was talented at assisting small businesses market their products. Arriving at Morehouse, I aimed to be a business major, with a concentration in marketing. It was my plan to use my degree to start my own marketing firm helping Black businesses.

By the time sophomore year came and I started taking business classes, I learned quickly that the business department didn't feel like home to me. At the time I didn't have suits to wear to class, I was more concerned with reading pop culture blogs than the *Wall Street Journal*, and I sucked at accounting. In my accounting class, I earned a D on the midterm, and for me that D said, "Don't Stay."

That same semester of my disastrous accounting class, I took Introduction to Television with Professor Adisa Iwa. Professor Iwa was a Morehouse graduate and was an incredible professor who always spoke life into me. He would always say, "Chris, you're gonna be super-duper mega successful in Hollywood."

Professor Iwa was a professor in the Cinema, Television and Emerging Media Studies (CTEMS) program at Morehouse. In this program, students are exposed to fundamental skills to start careers in the television and film industry. CTEMS majors are taught how to write screenplays, pitch ideas and analyze industry trends. My first taste of the program was Professor Iwa's Introduction to Television course. I earned an A+ on his midterm exam. After that D in Accounting, the A in Introduction to Television compelled me to change majors.

By my junior year I was majoring in Cinema, Television and Emerging Media Studies and taking drama classes at Spelman College. I wasn't sure what my plan would be, but I imagined that synthesizing these two departments would give me some direction as to what I should do for a career. With the change of my major, my grades improved. It was after I changed my major that I landed really cool internships. I worked at 20th Century FOX as an audience strategy intern. Junior year I was a Production Intern on *The Tonight Show Starring Jimmy Fallon*. During my senior year, I had the great honor of being a talent acquisition intern for Turner at the CNN Center.

Working on the FOX lot in Los Angeles, 30 Rockefeller in Manhattan, and the CNN Center in Atlanta by my last semester of college gave me an in-depth view of what the entertainment industry was like. I learned how a show is marketed, how a show is produced for live television, and the complete process of on-boarding new talent to a company. When graduation came, I felt I could get any job that I desired.

Morehouse taught me that low aim is sin, so with that in mind I planned to work at the Oprah Winfrey Network in West Hollywood. I printed out the logo and placed it above my dorm room door because I wanted to remind myself that every time I walked out of my room I was walking one step closer to OWN. I had no plan how I was going to work for OWN or even what my job title would be; I just wanted to see if it was possible. First, I started working on my résumé. Second, I asked all my professors if they knew anyone at OWN. Third, I got on LinkedIn and began cold messaging, adding any OWN employee I could find. After several weeks, a LinkedIn friend informed me that OWN was in the middle of a hiring freeze.

At the time, I didn't even know what a hiring freeze was. I was told hiring freezes occur when a company temporarily stops non-essential hiring to reduce costs. Hiring freezes can be short term or long term and take place to avoid laying off current employees. Upon hearing this news, I completely lost all hope of working for OWN post-graduation. By this time, it was the spring of 2017, and graduation was just a few weeks away. I had no time to wait for a hiring freeze to end– I needed a job, and fast. I didn't want to be one of those graduates who returned home. I wanted to have something to do.

A part of my desire to find a job was that I felt that this was the only right move following college. Another part of me was trying to land a job because of what other people would think of me. I had built a reputation on campus for snagging cool internships. I had the résumé, the communication skills, and the talent to get any job I desired. There was no way that I, Chris Sumlin, should struggle to get a job. My ego was the driving force of my goal. Instead of desiring to work a job where I could take care of myself and use what I learned in school, I wanted to land a job so I could have something to talk about around campus.

Oprah defines the ego as "any self-identification with form." When we begin to wrap our identity with the jobs we work, the degrees we have earned, or the car we drive, our ego-self starts taking over. My ego-self told me that because I went to Morehouse and held down good internships that I needed a post-grad full time job to feel fulfilled. Iyanla Vanzant defines ego as "edging God out." When we sit in our egos, we edge God out and diminish our true selves.

For me, my true self was a man who enjoyed showing up with excellence and being myself. That true self allowed me to authentically come across to recruiters and land opportunities. By my senior year when my ego-self began to take over, my desire to be excellent and follow my passion transformed to desperation. I was taking that desperate, ego energy into my job search.

As my senior year began to wind down and I knew that I wasn't going to be able to work at OWN, I began praying. My spiritual practice drastically increased. I began reading my Bible more and praying that God would give me some sort of direction.

The Bible says in Matthew 7:7, "Ask and it will be given to you; seek and you will find; knock and the door will be opened to you." I began asking God for His will to be done in my life. I can't lie. During this time I experienced a little anxiety. I was unsure of what I was going to do next. In the midst of this struggle I learned of the Bible verse 1 Peter 5:7 which says, "Cast all your anxiety on Him because He cares for you." This scripture helped medicate my anxiety. As I kept praying and kept believing, my anxiety was replaced with peace.

One weekend a close friend came to campus to visit. Russell Pointer Jr. graduated from Morehouse in 2016 and was someone I had known since my last year of high school. Because he too had come down to Morehouse from a religious family, Russell was like a mentor who showed me how to navigate the campus. He was someone I always went to when I needed support or advice. When Russell came down to campus, he was already a Morehouse graduate and finishing up his first year of graduate school at the University of Tennessee-Knoxville. Upon hearing my frustrations about my post graduate plans, Russell suggested that I consider going to graduate school.

Graduate school had never crossed my mind. I was satisfied that graduating from Morehouse would be the end to my higher education journey. Russell felt differently.

Russell compelled me and almost harassed me to look up graduate programs. Earning a bachelor's in Cinema, Television and Emerging Media Studies, I was unsure of what type of graduate work I would study–I figured maybe an MFA in screenwriting or some type of fine arts master's degree. Together we searched on Google for television master's programs, and we looked at a few different schools on the web: New York University, Pepperdine, and UCLA, to name a few. Eventually we found a master's program in television available at Boston University. My degree program at Morehouse was dedicated to both television and film studies. I always enjoyed my television courses more than my film ones. Knowing that I would be able to earn a master's degree in television exclusively was the selling point for me.

Applying to colleges takes a lot of time, effort, energy, and money. It was never my plan to go to graduate school in the first place, and I was running out of time, so I applied to only one program, the program at Boston University. There was something about getting a master's degree in television that felt right. I wasn't getting a degree in film studies, or screenwriting. I was getting a Master of Science in Television. The degree name alone gave me the push I needed to apply to Boston University and Boston University only.

Offered through BU's College of Communication, the television master's program had two degree concentrations. I pursued the producing and management concentration. This track was dedicated to teaching students how to produce television and become thriving executives in the entertainment industry. Since I had learned a decent amount about screenwriting at Morehouse, I felt that the producing and management track would be a more suitable option for me.

After my weekend conversation with Russell, I began working my hardest to gather the necessary materials to officially apply. I wrote my essays, curated my transcripts, and got my letters of recommendations from esteemed members of the Morehouse community. I didn't think that I would get accepted because Boston University was such a good school, but I at least wanted to apply. I told my parents that if I applied and was accepted, I would go, but if I wasn't accepted, then I knew that wasn't meant to be. At least I would have tried. While applying to Boston University, I still kept my spiritual practice intact. I was still praying, still believing, and knew that my fate was in God's hands.

So much about the Boston University application process was seamless. My application essays were fun to write and were reflective of my story telling ability. I was given the money to pay for my official transcripts to be sent. The school even waived my application fee. When I sent my application over, I felt good knowing that whatever the outcome would be, I had given it my best.

Once my application was submitted, I emailed Professor Garland Waller, the head of the television program. I expressed to her my deep interest in being considered for the BU program. I also asked if any Morehouse graduates ever had enrolled in the television program. Her email was so warm and kind. In her response, she told me that I would be the first Morehouse alum to enroll in her program. After our email exchange, I began to feel even more excited about what was to come. I just knew that I would be accepted and that everything would work out.

It was the first week of May. Finals week had just ended, and the anxiety of finishing college was at an all-time high. One day I was hanging with one of my classmates, Marvin. We were having a good conversation, catching up, when I felt convicted to check my email. Upon refreshing my messages, I saw a congratulatory message from Boston University expressing that I had been accepted. Not only was I accepted, but I also was placed on an academic scholarship. My heart beamed with joy! I knew that my acceptance to BU was meant to be.

After getting the news, I began telling everyone who would listen about how I got accepted into a graduate program. I knew my acceptance gave me a clear sense of direction of what I was going to do next after undergrad. I was so proud of myself. My fear of not knowing what to do was gone; my desire to land a job for ego purposes was eradicated. I had found my next step.

I was twenty-three at the time of my acceptance into Boston University. This story taught me the importance of having faith and following your own path. How often do we slip and fall into the trap of comparing ourselves to others, and acting out of our egos? How easy is it to fall victim to the pressure of having it all together at all times? Sometimes life gives us a clear, definitive path of what to do next, and sometimes it doesn't. I went weeks trying to manifest a goal for myself that wasn't even mine. Had I landed my job at OWN, I wouldn't have been accepted into graduate school in Boston. I would have had a completely different experience and be on a different path. My biggest lesson that I learned from this experience is to trust life.

Trust is a firm belief in the reliability, truth, ability, or strength of someone or something. I had to get out of the space of my ego and land into trust—trust in myself that I would do the work necessary to accomplish my goals and trust in God that it would all work out for the best. I truly believe that our lives are already predestined for us before we are even born. Although we may have our goals, plans, or desires, God always has a bigger goal waiting for us. We just have to be open-minded enough to receive it.

Faith without works is dead. I had the faith that something good was coming my way, and I did the work that it took to bring that something to life. This is how I have learned to tackle every obstacle and goal. I have my idea of what I want to do, but then I surrender it to God. I try my hardest to do everything in my power to bring that goal to life, and then I surrender it knowing that whatever is meant to happen, will happen.

This notion of trying, failing, and believing is simple in theory but hard in practice. It is hard to work at something and then it does not work out. It is difficult to try and fail. But the reward that comes with sticking to a goal and rising above the adversity no matter what is so fulfilling.

If there ever comes a time where you are unsure of what to do next:

- Get still.
- Get focused.
- Start trying things.

Allow your life to unfold as it is supposed to even if that plan is different than what you had envisioned. Trust your journey.

CHAPTER 6
Confidence in Class

When you have confidence, you can have a lot of fun.
And when you have fun, you can do amazing things.
–Joe Namath

COURTNEY E. ACKERMAN is a psychology researcher and holds a master's degree in Positive Organizational Psychology from Claremont Graduate University. In an article for PositivePsychology.com, Ackerman writes:

> Studies have confirmed that self-esteem has a direct relationship with our overall well-being, and we would do well to keep this fact in mind—both for ourselves and for those around us, particularly the developing children we interact with.

Healthy self-esteem is an aspect of life that so many of us struggle to obtain. It is important to discuss self-esteem and self-confidence in this chapter in order to provide practical steps to becoming a more confident person. Whether looking to land a promotion, develop a personal brand, or spice up your love life, possessing self-confidence can be an essential tool to getting you where you want to be in life.

Like many others, I've struggled with self-confidence, but luckily, I've had to learn quickly how to make my presence known and build my self-esteem. No greater experience taught me how to do this than starting graduate school.

On August 30, 2017, I began my journey in Boston, Massachusetts. At the time I was twenty-three years old. I was living in a party house in Allston, Massachusetts, with a barrage of roommates. Our house was so big and full of life and vibrant personalities. Some days I would lock myself in my room and read a book or listen to music. Other days I really enjoyed exploring the city. Boston had a freshness to it and a vibe that I really enjoyed. The city is an epicenter for higher education. In close proximity of schools such as Boston College, MIT, Emerson, and of course, Harvard, I felt like I was surrounded by young ambitious students looking to change the world.

The twenties are an age of self-exploration and adventure. When I landed in Boston to start my graduate schoolwork, that was my first time truly experiencing the city and my campus. Before being admitted to Boston University, I had never visited BU's campus or been to Boston for a long period of time. There was a lot I did not know, but I was eager to learn and try new things.

In any new situation self-identity is essential to success. When I was in a new city, surrounded by new people, it would have been fairly easy for me to become overwhelmed and get lost. Not lost in a sense of my geographical location, although that might have been likely too. I mean lose who I was or who I thought I was at that time.

I remember taking a course called Media Evolution taught by two esteemed Boston University professors, Cathy Perron and Will Richmond. The course was mandatory for our entire graduate school program cohort. Regardless of concentration, career interest, or track, every student was required to take Media Evolution. It was offered only in the fall, so all of the students in my program took this particular class all at the same time.

Walking into the class I was amazed at how diverse the class was demographically. There were about forty of us in the class—mostly women, including women of color, a few men, and four Black men. Of course, BU wasn't like Morehouse. I was used to my entire class being Black men. This was different.

When class began, the two instructors introduced themselves. Early on I understood that although both Cathy and Will were kind professors, they also meant business. I figured this was not going to be an easy class if I didn't show up and do my absolute best. After explaining the course, going over the syllabus, and doing the regular first day of class rituals, Professor Perron started to take attendance.

As she went around the room, everyone stated their name, where they were from, and how to pronounce their name. When she got to the last names beginning with S, my heart started beating; I was nervous. I knew that this would be the first impression that I would make on my entire graduate program. I didn't want to come across as anything less than confident, intelligent, and friendly.

"Christopher Sumlin."

"That's me!" I replied with a big smile and raised my hand.

"Do you go by Christopher?"

"I actually go by Chris Sumlin—one word, like Mariah Carey or Donald Trump."

Some of my classmates began to laugh. With a warm smile Professor Perron said, "Ah! You already got your Hollywood name. I love it." I smiled as she moved on to the next name.

That small instance was a defining moment for me. When I graduated from Morehouse, I began to move through the world with confidence. No matter where I was, who I was with, or what I was doing, I did my best to always make sure that I was present and that my presence was respected.

When I was younger there were moments where I struggled to be present and make myself known. I had a lot of insecurities as a teenager. It was hard for me to introduce myself and be confident. I think we all go through those weird stages in our lives when things just don't add up and we may feel insecure. Once I truly started to appreciate and honor myself at all times, my experience began to change.

Every thought, action, and word we speak over ourselves has power. I was a person who loved to make self-deprecating jokes; I thought that made me humorous and likable. Unfortunately, those jokes used to eat away at my self-esteem on a subconscious level. There were moments when people would give me a compliment and I would deflect it with a joke or an insult. For instance, when someone would say, "Chris, I like your outfit," I would respond with, "Oh I just threw this on, you know. I can't dress that well."

After a while my words became my reality. I created an entire insecurity for myself because I kept telling myself a negative story about who I was and what my abilities were. We all have to make the effort to tell ourselves a positive, affirming story about who we are and allow the world to experience that confident person.

I believe in God. I believe that I was created with intention by the divine spirit. In my heart I feel like every complexity, quirk, and nuance that I have was made by God for a reason. When we dishonor, diminish, and disrespect ourselves, not only is that limiting to our own experiences, but it is disrespectful to God. It is disrespectful to our parents, our communities, and anyone who has ever invested anything in us at all.

Confidence and self-affirmation are rarely taught in pop culture. There is this notion of always downplaying who we are in the world with the hope of lifting other people up. This practice is backward. Marianne Williamson speaks on this in her best-selling book, *A Return to Love: Reflections on the Principles of "A Course in Miracles*. She writes:

> Our deepest fear is not that we are inadequate. Our deepest fear is that we are powerful beyond measure. It is our light, not our darkness that most frightens us. We ask ourselves, Who am I to be brilliant, gorgeous, talented, fabulous? Actually, who are you not to be? You are a child of God. Your playing small does not serve the world. There is nothing enlightened about shrinking so that other people won't feel insecure around you. We are all meant to shine, as children do. We were born to make manifest the glory of God that is within us. It's not just in some of us; it's in everyone. And as we let our own light shine, we unconsciously give other people permission to do the same. As we are liberated from our own fear, our presence automatically liberates others.

This one pivotal moment where I introduced myself to my class helped set the tone for the rest of the semester.

I was in a completely new environment, a tad nervous, and unsure of what my experience would bring, but I still managed to affirm myself in the most subtle but effective way.

Weeks later after one of our classes, my professor pulled me to the side to commend me on my presence in class. "I love how you put yourself out there. That's how you get noticed and get yourself a job. Keep up the good work." I took her advice and continued to be strong, present and confident. My confidence allowed me to make some really cool friends during my grad school program and even land a paid internship at Legendary Entertainment my last semester of graduate school. It pays to be confident. I invite you to try different affirming and positive ways to let people know who you are in any given situation.

Whenever I'm creating, writing, or speaking, my intention is always to allow those who experience my work to believe in two things. First, I desire to raise the consciousness of everyone I encounter to believe that the universe we participate in is a safe, fulfilling, and loving experience. Second, I desire to push people to believe in themselves regardless of whatever their situation may be.

I'm often asked, "Why do you call yourself 'The' Chris Sumlin? Who are you to call yourself that?"

"How do you speak so confidently in front of everyone no matter where you are?"

"How are you so confident?"

What I know for sure, is that the way you see yourself is the way that others will perceive you. If you think you aren't worthy of anything in this world, then others will treat you that way. The questions above are ones that I get all the time. Everywhere I go people comment on how confident I am. I've worked really hard at trying to become a confident person.

Like anyone else, I have my flaws, things about myself that I wish I could change and fears about how I'm perceived. But being confident is something I work to achieve daily. I believe that self-confidence is like a muscle. It is something you develop over time and work to maintain. I don't have it perfect yet, but I have some tips to get you well on your way to having supreme self-confidence.

1. Think of Yourself Less

Wow! How contradictory, right? There's a quote that reads, "Stop overthinking! You are only creating problems that aren't there!" This quote continually helps me with my self-confidence.

Whenever I'm at a conference or a panel discussion, I love asking questions during the Q&A portion. If you are ever at an event with me where there is an audience and a Q&A, you can best believe I'm asking one. Every time, I repeat, *every time* I get ready to ask a question, I get terrified. I start shaking, my palms sweat, and I get very nervous. The reason I panic is because I start overthinking. I wonder, "Who is *not* going to like my question?" "Will I sound dumb when I speak?" "What if I mess up?"

All of that overthinking causes fear and doubt in my mind. Thinking of myself less in these moments helps ease my self-doubt. Before I get to the microphone, I take a few deep breaths, ask my question, and go back to my seat. As soon as I start envisioning who might think my question was dumb or how bad my haircut is, I use this opportunity to think of myself less. When I step back and think of myself less, I can relax and not overthink my situation. As you experience your young adult life, never overthink your situation when it doesn't serve you. So often we can have a propensity to overthink and create a fictional narrative that will cause self-doubt or fear.

Fear can be understood as an acronym for *False Evidence Appearing Real.* As we sit and create false narratives about who we are because of what we think someone might think of us, that thinking allows for fear to creep in. In moments like these, take a breath, do your thing, and don't think of yourself so much.

2. Tell Yourself A Good Story

Being self-critical is one of the biggest hindrances to self-confidence. Don't be a person who makes self-deprecating jokes or talks to themselves negatively. Talk to yourself in a way that you would talk to someone you love.

Life is going to be hard enough. Whenever you attempt to do anything with your life, there will be turbulence and resistance there to test you and force you to grow. You never have to worry about life not giving you reasons to be humble. The opportunities to fail, be embarrassed, or humbled are ubiquitous. You have to fill yourself up and keep your cup full. Affirmations are effective; they will help you in your pursuit toward your goals.

Our country often forgets that President Barack Obama was not taken seriously in the early days of his presidential campaign. There were those who thought he was too Black, too young, and too ambitious to become the President of the United States. Although naysayers shared their opinions, and the opportunity to accept a false narrative about himself was there, President Obama always stayed focused. There was never a moment where Obama doubted himself publicly.

In a February 2007 *60 Minutes* interview, then-Senator Barack Obama was asked by journalist Steve Kroft if America was ready for a Black president. "Yes," Obama replied as he looked Kroft right in the eye. You could see the clear confidence in Obama's face. It was evident he believed in himself. President Obama's belief system carried him all the way to victory, and he became one of the most adored presidents of all time. We have to be like President Obama and tell ourselves a self-affirming story that can push us toward our goals in the face of adversity.

3. Surround Yourself with Good Company

The Bible says in Proverbs 13, "Whoever walks with the wise becomes wise, but the companion of fools will suffer harm." It is also important to surround yourself with good company. Good friends and good family will make you feel special even on your worst day.

When I was a teenager, I was always bullied. I was constantly told I was ugly and weird. I can't lie; I did have a lot working against me. As a kid, dressing well wasn't a priority. I was a kid who was super involved in church while at the same time adored Beyoncé. I never ran or worked out, so naturally I was chubby. Ages twelve through fourteen were some of my most insecure years. Every day I felt like a nobody. (Isn't that insane? Who would have ever thought?) As a youngin' I could have believed the people at my middle school who bullied me. Instead, I would listen to my grandmother who always told me I was handsome and special even when I thought I wasn't.

I encourage you to be mindful of the company you surround yourself with. Be extremely mindful of how they talk to you and about you. Even when people are joking with you, be cautious of the jokes that they make. If a friend's joke makes you feel down, call your friend out on it. You want to try to do your best to position yourself around those who are going to lift you up and root for your rise. If you find people who give you some sort of sincere encouragement every time you encounter them, honor it and keep those people around. Our lives are not games to be toyed with but an opportunity to add value to the universe. Get around people who honor you and allow you to be your highest and best self.

4. Invest in Yourself

Always invest in yourself; it's not selfish, it's self-love. Nothing makes me feel more confident than a new outfit I just bought, a haircut, or finishing a new book. When I take time for myself, I feel confident and good. There is nothing wrong with taking care of yourself first. Get haircuts, get manicures, exercise, and honor yourself. You cannot be of service to the world, your family, or your friends if you have nothing within yourself to offer. The way you carry yourself, dress, and move through the world will oftentimes speak for you before you even open your mouth. Be cognizant of the message you are sending out every time you walk out of the house. Ask yourself, "Is this the kind of message I am trying to send?" "Am I honoring myself by carrying myself in this way?"

I love sweatpants and sneakers just as much as the next guy. I love having my feet out and wearing flip flops with no socks because it is comfortable. As comfortable as it is, there are moments where I really have to put forth that extra effort and put on an outfit with actual shoes and socks. I have to make that effort to get a haircut. Self-maintenance and investing in ourselves is hard work, but the reward makes it all worth it.

5. Understand Your *You-ness*

According to the 2020 Census Bureau there, are over 330 million people in the US alone, but there is only one you. That is your power.

When something is rare and unique, that alone makes it valuable. Always understand that no matter who comes around and what happens, no one will ever be able to be another you! When you flow through life with that perspective, it will make you more confident.

Confidence is not something you get overnight, but with the right intention and practice, it can surely be obtained. If you apply these five tips to your life and use good judgment, you will have the self-confidence of a superstar before you know it. Start today and live unapologetically.

CHAPTER 7
Chris at Cane's

When you are committed, you do whatever it takes.
–Fabienne Fredrickson

ONCE I GOT INTO the swing of graduate school in Boston, I was unsure how to adjust to the heavy demands of my academic load and the city's high cost of living. No one had ever taught me about work-study programs or how to sustain income while being a graduate student. The only thing I knew was that I had rent due and I needed to find a way to pay it on time. I was renting a room in a house in Allston, and the room was about $700 a month. At the time I was twenty-three, and it was the first time I was ever responsible for paying rent. My parents were people who were always on time for rent. They set the example of how to be responsible adults. I knew that I wanted to be on time every time for rent, and because of that I needed a job.

It made no difference that I already had a college degree. I can't lie. I felt a bit of pressure after finishing Morehouse. I had friends who were working at LinkedIn, Google, and Oracle and making upwards of $60,000 a year. None of that mattered to me because I was still in graduate school. I knew that I needed a part time job to handle my living costs. My bigger concerns were where I would apply, what I would do, and how I would find a job that was part time and gave me the income to sustain my living but didn't interfere with my classes. To my benefit, Boston University had a job board where they would post open positions online exclusively for students.

Searching the website, I knew that half my battle was already won. I only needed to find a job that would work for me. About two days after continually checking the site for a potential position, I saw an opening for a crew member at Raising Cane's, a fast-food restaurant chain specializing in chicken fingers. This position seemed like a winner because it was paying $12 an hour, which at the time was the highest hourly wage I had ever been paid.

I calculated that if I worked just twenty hours out of the week at $12 an hour, my weekly salary would be $240, biweekly salary $480, and monthly salary $960. Taxes vary from state to state, but I knew that my rough estimate of $960 was enough for my $700 monthly rent.

One of the first jobs I ever held in high school was as a service champion at Taco Bell when I was seventeen. To this day, my job at Taco Bell is the longest I ever worked for a company; I was at Taco Bell for an entire year. The Taco Bell that I worked at was located on the corner of High Street and Hudson Avenue, right near the campus of The Ohio State University. We had a drive through, longer hours, and many intoxicated guests. There was even a customer who in her drunken state cussed me out in front of the entire store because she felt I was ignoring her. It was the only time in my life I had ever been called "bitch face" while at work. Raising Cane's seemed like an upgrade from my time at Taco Bell. My thinking was incredibly positive. I assumed I would work in the evenings away from my classes, serve esteemed Boston University students, and be able to afford my rent.

My interview went very well. I wore a button-up shirt, slacks, and a bright smile. Although I was a college graduate and a published author at the time, I did my best to focus on the fact that I simply needed to pay my bills. I sincerely wanted the job and did my best to leave my ego at the door for the interview. I vividly remember telling the hiring manager at Raising Cane's how I worked at Taco Bell in high school and how that made me an excellent hire for his team. He agreed, and I was hired on the spot. My job duties consisted of taking orders, cleaning the dining room, and supporting the team any way I could. My first few days at Raising Cane's were cool. I found the job to be very easy; all of the customers loved my positive attitude, and our dining room used to play a lot of Ariana Grande, which I learned to enjoy.

Working at Raising Cane's felt similar to my days at Taco Bell. It was expected that we all would work our best to assist each other, get along, and get the job done. The biggest difference was that this time I was one of the oldest people on my team. All of the other crew members were still undergrads trying to find their way. When the store wasn't as busy, and small talk would occur, I did my best to talk less and listen more. I kept my head down and worked hard.

At the time I started working at Raising Cane's, I was proud of myself because I knew I was making an honest living and doing what I needed to do. It was also incredibly helpful that my manager would let us take food home, so I never went hungry. I knew I could always get a chicken finger plate whenever I wanted. My weight was probably the highest it had ever been because it was nothing to eat chicken tenders throughout the entire shift and then take as many tenders home as we wanted with lots of fries and sauce. The lemonade was a treat too, made of just water, lemons, and sugar—no artificial ingredients. Every sip was better than the last. A cool, refreshing cup of Cane's lemonade in the hot kitchen reminded me of Atlanta.

On one end, I felt good because I was working hard and paying my bills. On the other end, I felt this deep shame that I was working at a fast-food restaurant. During my time at Raising Cane's, I had a book on Amazon, I had another book in production, and most notably, I was a Morehouse Man. I had this narrative in my mind that Morehouse Men are expected to do well.

Theodore Roosevelt once said, "Comparison is the theft of joy," and boy, was he correct. Scrolling through Instagram, I saw my classmates working at great companies such as IBM, Google, and LinkedIn. My friends seemed to be doing well, thriving in their respective cities, and here I was alone in Boston serving chicken tenders. The shame sat on my mind every day I clocked in. Each day I held my breath, praying that none of my grad school classmates or even worse, my professors would come into the restaurant. I didn't want anyone to know that I was working at a chicken finger joint. The shame I felt also silenced me. I never once told my coworkers what I had done or even that I was in graduate school. Each shift, I would simply do my job, keeping all of my accolades and ambitions to myself.

When people asked me what I studied, I simply stated that I was in the college of communication. I told everyone that I was in the TV and film program. It was very easy to hide everything that I had done. None of my coworkers followed me on LinkedIn or Instagram. I don't even recall telling people my last name. I was just Chris, the guy who was really good at taking orders and sang along to the radio throughout my shifts. I told only my parents and close friends that I worked at Raising Cane's. Today, as I write these very words, I can't find one single photo of me on the internet or on my phone of me working at Raising Cane's. As a person who posts on social media daily and shares their life, this fact is shocking. I guess I was even trying to convince myself that working at Raising Cane's never happened. As much shame and disappointment as I felt for myself at that time, my bills were paid.

Never during my time as a Raising Cane's crew member was my phone ever disconnected or was I late for rent. My calculations were correct and allowed me to even have a little bit of extra money to be able to buy groceries and even have my laundry paid for, which is one of my favorite guilty pleasures. There is a confidence that comes with having enough to live. In college, I always felt like I never really had enough. In undergrad, it was a lot to try to keep up with everyone else, go out to all of the events, and keep my haircut. When I was working at Raising Cane's, it was the first time I felt like I was a man, taking care of myself. My mom would always tell me how proud she was that I was handling my business as a man. She used to say to me there was nothing nobler than a working Black man doing his best to survive.

Although I was working at Raising Cane's, I also made a concerted effort to make the best out of the situation. At nights when I would close the shift and was expected to clean the dining room, I listened to podcasts as I mopped the floor. Boston University has a large international student population, so when students with Asian names came into the restaurant, I did my best to learn their names and ask questions about their culture. I worked hard at making sure I was making the best out of what could have been a pitiful situation.

What my time at Raising Cane's taught me was that it is okay to do what you have to do until you can do what you want to do. In life, there may come moments where you have to do things that are uncomfortable, unorthodox, or maybe even embarrassing. It is okay to do things that don't look cute on Instagram. Sometimes you may have to do something uncomfortable on your way toward your goals. Today, people are losing their jobs left and right, and I know that there are individuals who may have to work a job that they aren't comfortable with working, but it is okay. Sometimes you do what you have to do to survive, and that is nothing to be ashamed of.

As I was a young child growing up, my dad worked at a slew of fast-food restaurants as a general manager. There were even moments when he couldn't find anyone to watch us, so my three siblings and I would go to the restaurant dining room and occupy ourselves until Dad got off work. Although at the time my dad was a man of God, a minister, and the founder of a new church, he still did what he had to do to provide for his family.

Orlando, my oldest brother, began working in high school. He was very popular at his high school because he went to a performing arts school and was an incredibly talented singer. The first job Orlando worked was at Taco Bell.

He was actually the reason that I was able to get a job at the same Taco Bell when I was old enough. Although Orlando was popular, talented, and was doing very well in high school, it was his plan to work at Taco Bell to save money before he went to college. When Orlando began working, he didn't have a car to drive his way to work each day, so he rode the bus. Day in and day out I never saw my brother complain. He was a prime example of doing what you have to do until you can do what you want to do.

Self-confidence is great. I always want people to believe in themselves, but there is a stark contrast between having self-confidence and an ego. Ego is that loud voice in your head that tells you when you are too good, too cool, or better than a situation.

It was my ego that would creep up and tell me, "You should be ashamed of yourself for working at a fast-food restaurant."

It was self-confidence that said, "You should be proud of yourself for making an honest living."

It was my ego that would say, "Look at you on the bus. How pathetic. You should have a car like your other friends."

It was self-confidence that said, "I'm on the bus, but I'm doing what I have to do for myself without any help, and that is something to be proud of."

Both voices were looking at the exact same situation but with two different lenses. We must always be cognizant of the voices that we allow to have power and dominion over our lives. The self-confidence voice that I learned to listen to served me a lot more than my ego telling me I should be doing more or better. I kept pushing and did my best at Raising Cane's and was able to make my rent because I did what it took to make it happen.

I love that quote that says, "You have to want to be successful as bad as you want to breathe." In the beginning when I heard that quote, I thought that it was a tad dramatic. What I have come to learn is just how powerful that mantra really is. When we have our goals, tasks, and desires, we have to want to accomplish them as badly as we want to breathe. We can't be cute with it, play with it, or expect that whatever we desire to accomplish may be easy. We have to want it as badly as we want to breathe. We have to attack our goals at whatever cost and do whatever it takes.

It disappoints me when I come across people who will articulate a goal, but when they learn what the goal will take, they run scared, not willing to put in that work. These are the people who are not willing to do what it takes. I wrote my second book, *Dealing with This Thing Called College,* while at home from Morehouse after graduation. At my mother's house, the only computer I had access to was an old desktop computer with Windows XP software on it. The computer was so outdated that I was unable to download Microsoft Word onto the system. I used Google Docs instead and continued to write my book on the old computer. Although I had limited resources and didn't have access to a MAC computer, I did what it took.

Now I must caution you not to think that doing whatever it takes means you will do *anything* it takes. There should never be a moment when you compromise your morals, values, or self-worth for anything. In this book, I often talk about vision; it is a mandate that you have a vision for yourself of what you will and will not tolerate.

I've had people offer me opportunities to sell drugs and middleman transactions. With social media marketing and Ponzi schemes on the rise, it's also become easier than ever to scam folks. Integrity is a core value of mine. If I have to deceive someone in order to make a quick buck, it's not for me. I understand that sometimes you have to do what it takes to survive, but it is important to have limits of things you just won't do. For me, working at a fast-food restaurant and riding the city bus is not a non-negotiable. Find what your non-negotiables are and set clear boundaries as to what you are not willing to do.

It is also important that we debunk myths that after a certain age we are supposed to have everything together, because that is not true. Early adulthood is tough and there will be moments when you will have to do what it takes on your way to your goal.

Do Won Chang is the owner of the fastest growing fashion retailer, Forever 21. In his twenties, Chang worked three jobs to make ends meet. After living a life of poverty and neglect, Oprah Winfrey landed a job anchoring the six o'clock news in Nashville, making twenty-two thousand dollars a year in her twenties. JK Rowling, the billionaire mind behind the Harry Potter series, said she experienced great turbulence in her twenties. Rowling rode public transportation, was jobless, and was "as poor as it is possible to be in modern Britain, without being homeless." Each of these individuals struggled in their twenties but did what they had to do until they reached massive success. Life is tough and sometimes you may have to take a different path to begin adulthood. There is nothing wrong with that at all.

I went to Morehouse, a phenomenal school, and still was trying to find my way to adjust to life. The pressure to be perfect in the years of early adulthood is dehumanizing and anxiety-inducing. If you are a young adult struggling to find your way, I hope this story teaches you that it is entirely okay to struggle and do nontraditional things to make ends meet. I was a college graduate and published author on the bus, taking chicken finger orders. Of course there were moments where my ego got the best of me and made me feel bad, but I had to let my self-confidence speak louder and reaffirm that I was doing what it took to survive.

If you are a person who has lost their job and has to go work at a grocery store or do Postmates, that is okay too. We should applaud anyone who is working any honest job to provide for themselves and their families.

Sometimes surviving doesn't look as great as thriving, and there is nothing wrong with that. With all your goals, suspend your ego, hold tight to vision, and do whatever it takes to keep moving forward.

CHAPTER 8
Success Takes Time

You don't set out to build a wall. You don't say, "I'm going to build the biggest, baddest, greatest wall that's ever been built." You don't start there. You say, "I'm going to lay this brick as perfectly as a brick can be laid."

–Will Smith

FINISHING MY MASTER'S program at Boston University was one of my biggest accomplishments. I was the first person in my immediate family to get a master's degree. Since my program was only three semesters, I was done with the entire program at BU by December of 2018. At the completion of my program I was twenty-four years old with two books on Amazon and three college degrees. The last semester of my program ended in a bi-coastal experience that allowed me to live in Los Angeles occupying a beautiful Park La Brea Apartment that the school paid for. Once my program was over, I had to move out of my apartment and be a full adult.

This period of transition took a toll on me. School was over, my apartment was gone, and it was the end of the calendar year when companies are less likely to hire new talent. I battled anxiety wondering where I would live, where I would work, and how I would use my new degree in a meaningful way. Depression crept up on me because I would continually look at throwback photos of myself in grad school when I was living in my beautiful apartment and partying around LA. I tried so hard to keep the momentum going, but I lost steam.

With my back against the wall, I called Bobbette. She and Larry were like adoptive parents to me. I spent Thanksgiving with them and they took me grocery shopping and were the only source of family I had while on the West Coast. I expressed to Bobbette how I was eating $4 meal deals at Taco Bell because I wasn't working. I told her I was staying in the most affordable Airbnbs in Los Angeles and how I was all alone. Things were tough. This was the one time in my life I struggled to sleep because I just couldn't fathom how my entire world could have turned upside down so quickly. I didn't feel like myself. I knew that I was going through a storm and had no idea how to get out of it this time.

When Bobbette heard of my struggles, she quickly instructed me to pack my bags to spend time at her and Larry's home in Baldwin Hills. Upon my arrival, Larry, Bobbette's husband, offered me Popeyes and his son's old bedroom. Over fried chicken I lamented about my time in LA, how things had dried up, and how I was unsure of what to do next.

Larry advised that I return to the East Coast to be surrounded by my friends. I had told Larry about Corbin and how he was my best friend. Larry asked if Corbin would be okay with me coming to stay with him for a while to catch my breath and get on my feet. That day I went from being unsure where I would live in LA, experiencing mild panic attacks, to being fed Popeyes and having a flight to Atlanta the next morning. Larry paid for my flight all by himself without asking for anything in return.

That night I couldn't even sleep, but this time it wasn't because of anxiety. This time it was because of excitement. I cried tears of joy. I was safe, fed, and had a flight to look forward to in the morning. It was as if Larry and Bobbette had swept in and taken away all my troubles. In one day, everything had turned around. I stayed at Larry and Bobbette's house for one night and flew to Atlanta the next morning, Christmas Eve 2018. I'm not sure Larry and Bobbette will ever understand how their generosity impacted me that day. My heart was overwhelmed with joy.

When I got to Atlanta, Corbin graciously opened his home and allowed me to stay with him as I figured things out. There were good days and bad days. Some days I was feeling good that I was with my friends, and others where I felt like a failure for not knowing my next move. I didn't want to overwhelm Corbin, so I bounced between his house and my friend Sean's house. Sean was aware of everything that I was going through and did his best to support me.

This was a dark time because I had lost myself. I was no longer a grad student, I had no job, and I was living between my friends' couches. I was self-critical, constantly beating myself up about why I could not find a job in LA. It was also difficult to socialize because when people asked me what I was up to or how I was doing, I didn't know what to say. I wanted to be honest and say, "I wasn't able to get a job in LA, so now I'm depressed, anxious, and living on friends' couches." But instead, I would tell a partial truth and say that I was back in Atlanta to spend time with friends. It's so funny how we lie to ourselves and others to save face.

It was January 2019, and I had been living in Atlanta for a few weeks. My friends and I celebrated my twenty-fifth birthday with bar hopping and a small house party. In a time of uncertainty, I was still blessed to learn more about friends through living with them. We all had been through so much since leaving Morehouse. The conversations that we shared following our experience allowed us to all grow closer.

Following my birthday week, I started feeling homesick. It was good being around my friends for a while, but I felt something had to change. My anxiety worsened. I struggled to sleep. My heart rate was higher than normal. I felt so bad that I even went to an urgent care center in Atlanta for a checkup. The doctor who examined me confirmed what I suspected—I was dealing with a high amount of stress due to drastic life changes. In just a matter of months, my internship had ended, my grad program had ended, and I had moved from one side of the country to the other. After a few weeks in Atlanta, I knew that in order for me to truly get back into a positive mental space, it was imperative that I return home to Columbus, Ohio, to my mother's house. So, I left.

Back in Ohio, some aspects of my reality were different; others were the same. I had the support of my family, my talent, and a newly earned master's degree. What I didn't have was a job or a definitive plan. My plan after graduate school always had been to work in the entertainment industry. Even though I was in Ohio, each morning I would religiously log onto LinkedIn, looking for new job posts. Daily I would check in with former colleagues and classmates to see if anyone could help me find a position. Although my effort was apparent, opportunities still never seemed to show up.

I began to lose hope. One afternoon after a morning of digital networking and job applications, I decided I was going to bask in self-pity and binge-watch *Naruto*. What I have come to learn is that God gives us exactly what we need when we need it. After two episodes of *Naruto*, something compelled me to refresh my e-mail. When I opened my e-mail, I saw a note from an early college readiness program coordinator. I received the e-mail at exactly 2:43 p.m. on January 22.

The message was kind, concise, but most notably random. The message read, "We are planning to use your newest book in our summer transition class for these high school graduates, and it would be great for them to hear from the author. I can be reached by e-mail or phone to discuss speaking and travel fees."

Following the release of my first book in 2016, *Dealing with this Thing Called Life*, I began booking speaking gigs in Ohio and Georgia. My former teachers loved having me come to talk to their students. The United Negro College Fund allowed me to speak at banquet events for their donors, which gave me awesome opportunities to share my story on corporate stages. Once I started graduate school, however, all of the public speaking took a pause. I put my speaking gigs and books on the back burner. I was more interested in working for someone else in the entertainment industry than in doing my own thing as a speaker-author. It was almost as if I had forgotten that I was a speaker or an author.

I read the e-mail five times before it dawned on me that this coordinator had become familiar with my book *Dealing with this Thing Called College*. Jumping with joy, I quickly responded to the e-mail, and later that week we talked on the phone. "Well, Mr. Baxter, how did you find me?" I hesitantly asked. "Well, I was Googling college readiness books. I found your website, read the free chapter of your book online, and decided this is the kind of material our students need."

My heart beamed with pride. This man had no idea that I was going through a rough patch at the time of his call. He was unaware of the mental state I was in and how discouraged I felt about my career that particular day. Our conversation was what I needed to help cheer me up. Months later, I traveled to the campus of the early college program in Raleigh, North Carolina, and had a phenomenal time. They allowed me to fly whatever airline I preferred, and I stayed in a nice Airbnb. The entire flight I couldn't help but feel what an honor it was to be flown into a city to share my story in front of the students. It was a dream come true.

On the day of our event, I met so many promising students and their parents and signed a slew of books that the school purchased. In my speech I talked about the importance of believing in yourself and working hard to get through college. As I was speaking, I could see how appreciative the students and staff were. The energy in the room healed me. The event blessed me in more ways than I could ever articulate. I was well compensated for my speech and told we would work together again soon.

My intent in telling this story is not to brag or boast. There are two big lessons that I have come to accept that I must share. The first is that God gives us what we need when we need it. It is imperative that we trust our path and journey. It was in the midst of my sadness that an opportunity fell in my lap. This entire situation reminded me how important it is to trust the timing of life and to not be anxious.

The other teachable nugget here is to stress how important it is to work hard, start small, and dream big. My second book, *Dealing with this Thing Called College*, was written because I felt like I had a story to share. I knew first-hand how hard it was for me, a first-generation college student, to graduate from college. The day after graduation, I started writing because doing so felt like purpose-driven work. Not once did I think about who would buy the book or how many speaking engagements I could snag; I merely wanted to share my story. I didn't know that I would still be landing opportunities for myself from that one book months later. I only knew that I had a project that I was passionate about creating.

Passion should always be the driving force in anything that you desire to do. It shouldn't be money or sales or anything like that. When you allow yourself to listen to the utterance of your heart and create good work, you will be paid as a result.

Shawn Jay-Z Carter is one of the most successful rappers of all time. In interviews, Jay-Z often states how, unlike most rappers who read from notes, he can rap off the top of his head. He says that when he was growing up in Marcy

Projects in Brooklyn, he enjoyed going around the neighborhood rapping against guys on the block. As a young kid, Jay-Z rapped because he truly loved it. I highly doubt that in his early twenties Jay-Z was rapping because he thought it would make him a billionaire or that it would position him to marry Beyoncé. He was rapping because he loved it. That is how we all should be. We should be people who use our natural gifts because we simply love doing it.

In Zechariah 4:10, the Bible says, "Do not despise these small beginnings, for the Lord rejoices to see the work." So often, in our social media culture, everyone wants to see quick, instantaneous results of their work. People expect to have that viral success, that one song that changes their lives, or that one video that gives them national press. Rarely do careers that last a long time have this quick, microwaveable success. Good work takes time, and you may not see the fruits of your labor quickly.

Take the singer Mariah Carey for example. In December of 2019, *Billboard* reported that Mariah Carey had become the first artist to top the Hot 100 in four distinct decades (notably, with a song from the 1990s extending her run into both the 2010s and 2020s). With nineteen Hot 100 number 1 hits, Mariah is considered the best-selling female artist of all time. When Mariah first started out, this wasn't her ultimate goal. When asked how it makes her feel to be the top-charting female solo artist in history Mariah said, "I never, ever dreamt of this when I first started. I just wanted to hear my songs on the radio." Mariah started writing songs in her teenage years, and it took lots of hard work and time before she experienced the massive success that she has today.

It was two years after I put down the first sentence of my book that I landed a four-figure fee speaking gig. Patience takes the cake every time. It is vital that we all continuously remind ourselves that any level of success takes time. It is okay to be patient, and it is okay to start small because good things take time to grow.

This idea of having patience is reflected in nature. Science tells us that the apple tree starts producing fruit after two to ten years depending on the type of rootstock grown from the seed. Good things take time to grow and change.

What I've learned from this experience is that if I just keep working hard over time and being true to my soul, the opportunities I seek will also seek me. The same is true for you.

I did impressive work by writing a book. My hard work continued when I built an SEO-friendly WordPress site that allowed me to show up on Google when someone searched for college readiness material. I can't count the number of hours it took to teach myself web design and the SEO tips I have implemented. The energy of all of those efforts met me when this coordinator found my work online and decided he wanted to work with me. We must continue to do work, regardless of who appreciates us now. The law of conservation of energy tells us that energy is neither created nor destroyed, rather, it can only be transformed or transferred from one form to another. We all have to trust that the energy, passion, and work that we put into whatever it is that we are doing will meet us in a positive, abundant way.

The Bible states in Galatians 6:7, "Whatsoever a man soweth, that shall he also reap." Whether you believe science or biblical scripture, the idea of getting out what we put in is supported by both sides of the spectrum. We all have to keep following our hearts and doing good work. As I reflect on this story, I am inspired. I plan to keep doing what feels right in my soul and trusting that everything else will work itself out. I desire to use my storytelling abilities to change the hearts and minds of those who will listen. Whether it is writing blogs, creating television, authoring a book, or recording a podcast, I will keep going even if it takes time before I see success. I hope after reading this story you feel the same way.

CHAPTER 9
Breaking Away

Consider it all joy, my brethren, when you encounter various trials, knowing that the testing of your faith produces endurance.

–St. James

IN THE SPRING OF 2018, I was afforded the opportunity to do some marketing consulting for two non-profit companies based in Decatur, Georgia. The companies were run by the Bugg family. Together the Bugg family had created Reaching Our Sisters Everywhere Inc. (ROSE) and Reaching Our Brothers Everywhere Inc. (ROBE). ROSE was founded to address breastfeeding disparities for communities of color and works to normalize breastfeeding by providing resources and networking opportunities for individuals and communities. ROBE seeks to educate, equip, and empower men to impact an increase in breastfeeding rates and a decrease in infant mortality rates within African American communities.

One of my Morehouse classmates told the Bugg family about my website and social media presence, and they asked me to join their team to help maintain their online marketing efforts. Once again, an opportunity had found me. Working with the Bugg family and the ROSE/ROBE team was a joy. Everyone who worked with the non-profits was so friendly, warm, and good at what they did. When I moved back to Atlanta after finishing graduate school, I was able to work with the team directly instead of through e-mails as we had done while I was in graduate school at Boston University (BU). Quickly everyone on the team became like family to me.

During my short time in Atlanta after finishing my program at BU, I would travel to Decatur and sit with the team, and we would work as hard as we could. At the beginning of 2019, I was informed that the ROSE/ROBE team was going to do a big summit to bring together all of their donors. Dr. Kimari Bugg, founder of ROSE, told me how vital it was that I attend the summit. I promised her that no matter where I was or what I had going on, I would make sure I was there to experience the 2019 Rose Summit in August.

Although I was living in Ohio, I knew that I was still going to attend the ROSE/ROBE Summit and that it would be exciting for me. During this time, I still wasn't working in my field or using my television master's degree, but I was in a much better head space than I had been.

The summer of 2019 was a comfortable time while I looked for a job in my field. Ohio was home but didn't have the job opportunities I was looking to snag. When I would tell my family and friends about my aspirations to work in TV, they would advise me to work for the local news. Working in the news was not something I wanted to do at all. I wanted to assist TV producers and work my way up, which meant working production assistant jobs and being on TV show sets. Following graduate school and everything that I had learned, I always understood that if I was going to work in the TV producing space, the only place I could do that was in Los Angeles. Although I had spent time in Atlanta and Columbus, I always told myself that I was merely visiting because Los Angeles was where I longed to be.

During those summer months, I spent time with my oldest brother Orlando, his then-wife Terri, and son, Tyson. Terri was very nice to me and was very supportive of my ambitions to live in Los Angeles. We used to go to the Crunch Gym together at all hours of the day and spend our time doing positive activities that I enjoyed. Terri also is an excellent cook, so every night we had great meals. Terri was aware of my passion for reading and how I really enjoyed college. I think we had a mutual respect for one another.

She was kind enough to even let me watch her seven-year-old son Tyson. Tyson was my little road dog during the summer of 2019. We were best friends. Being around Tyson was fun because he had great energy and a big personality. Our days consisted of movies, trips to Wendy's, and lots of ice cream. I also helped Tyson with his schoolwork. The highlight of my summer was helping Tyson with his reading. Tyson was a very active child and smart. Together we would sit and read Bible stories and books on Martin Luther King Jr., and we would walk to the library.

Kids are very honest. I remember a few times when Tyson would ask me what I was doing with my life because I didn't have a wife, a car, or a job. I would always respond by asking Tyson to pray for me and trust that God would help me find those things. Tyson would always pray, "God, please let Chris get a job so he can pay his bills and get his own house." It was hilarious.

As much as I was spending time with Tyson, I still had my goal in the forefront of my mind. I wanted to get back to Los Angeles and get a job, but I had no idea how it was going to happen.

In my experience, I never make a big decision without asking God for a clear sign. Throughout my months living in Ohio with Orlando, Terri, and Tyson, I kept asking God for a sign about where I should work or what I should do. I knew that I desired to work in the entertainment industry, but again, I had no idea how I would be able to do that. It was clear to me that I needed a practical, solid first step, but what that would be, I wasn't sure.

One day while spending time with Tyson, we decided to go to the library. The library is where I learned to read growing up, so I felt like a library day with Tyson would be beneficial for him too. Tyson was a tad fussy that day. He really didn't feel like going to the library. He made it very clear that he would much rather go for ice cream, but he followed my lead anyway.

Together we walked a mile to the Livingston Branch Library located on East Livingston Avenue. Walking through the library, I wanted to look at books first in the adult section of the library before I took Tyson to the children's section. I didn't have a plan to look for any book in particular, just browse. Something kind of took over me as I was walking through the book aisles. As I walked, something kept pushing me further and further into this particular aisle of books. As I was walking through the library, I looked to the left, and a book grabbed my attention. It was *Powerhouse: The Untold Story of Hollywood's Creative Artists Agency.*

I was familiar with Creative Artists Agency (CAA) because I knew that it was one of the most prominent talent agencies in the entertainment business. CAA represents clients such as Mariah Carey, Brad Pitt, Ariana Grande, and even Beyoncé. I was also aware that one of my former classmates, Justin Browning, worked at CAA. Seeing this book at the East Livingston library was the sign I needed to figure out the next step in my career journey.

> *I saw the sign, and it opened up my eyes.*
> *I saw the sign.*
> > –Ace of Base

At the time, I didn't think that anyone on East Livingston Avenue was thinking about CAA. Seeing this book randomly on the shelf on that day reassured me that God was speaking to me instructing me to work at CAA. I don't even recall staying at the library with Tyson that day. I just remember telling him that we needed to go home immediately.

That week I knew inside myself that I was going to work at CAA. I wasn't particularly excited about it, but I knew that it was predestined because I saw the sign. The first step in my plan to land at CAA was to call my former classmate Justin. I have a lot of respect for Justin, and I knew he could assist me in making my move to CAA. Justin is super smart, knows the ins and outs of Hollywood, and is respected by all those he encounters. Calling Justin, I already knew what God had shown me at the library, but I still wanted Justin's approval and support. Justin and I talked, and he explained to me what CAA was all about from the inside. He told me working at CAA would be an excellent move since CAA is the epicenter of the entertainment industry. Justin and I made it very clear that I was not going to be a talent agent, which was the usual career trajectory at CAA. We also understood that I probably wouldn't even stay there very long. The goal was to get inside CAA, meet as many people as I could, learn about the industry, and try to make genuine friends. The conversation I had with Justin was reaffirming. He then told the HR team at CAA about me. Quickly things began to unfold, and I was booked for a preliminary interview.

Although my plan to go to CAA was set, I still had no idea how I would get to LA, interview in person, and put my plan into action. With that said, I put CAA in the back of my mind and continued my summer as usual.

When August rolled around, Wesley Bugg, one of the members of the ROSE/ROBE team, called me and discussed how the team was going to fly me from Ohio to Atlanta to help with the ROSE Summit. He explained to me how a lot of great speakers would be coming into town. There would be lots of panel discussions, and we needed all hands on deck to make sure things flowed smoothly. I was determined to give the ROSE Summit my best and do all I could to help out. Following that phone conversation with Wesley, he booked me a flight from Columbus to Atlanta to make sure I was in town for the summit. My travel arrangements were confirmed on August 10, 2019. I was twenty-five years old.

The understanding was that I would fly from Columbus down to Atlanta to help with the ROSE Summit and then fly back home. The summit was from August 21 to August 23. I was expected to stay in a hotel provided by the ROSE/ROBE team, help out the entire summit, and then return home to Columbus. Once everything was booked and set in stone, I was very excited. It had been a few months since I had been in Atlanta. The last time I flew into Atlanta

I was struggling with depression after not being able to find work in LA. This trip to Atlanta would be far different.

Knowing that I would have a flight to Atlanta and a hotel, I instantly told my Morehouse brothers. It was my plan to help out with the summit as much as I could during the day and see as many of my friends as I could in the evening. My plan was set, until it wasn't.

On August 16, just a few short days before the summit, I woke up very early around 4:00 a.m. The house was quiet, no one was up yet, but I was up with my thoughts. I went to the bathroom to begin getting ready for the day when I felt a strong urge to change my ROSE/ROBE Summit flight. This feeling, this inclination, this epiphany felt compelling and almost overwhelming. I have no other way to describe this moment than as the voice of God. I felt that God was telling me to change my flight. I had a roundtrip flight from Columbus to Atlanta. This voice, this feeling, instructed me to change my final destination from Columbus to Los Angeles: "Fly from the summit to LA. Change your flight and hit the ground running."

Mind you, I didn't have any money saved up to relocate from Ohio to Los Angeles. I was getting money here and there by helping people with different projects, but not once was I making a solid living, especially one that would support me on the West Coast. Looking at the situation, it made no sense to just up and move to LA. At the time, I had no place to live, not a single suit, or even a plan. Why would I put myself in that situation and jump to LA?

What I have come to learn in life is that when God places ideas and plans into our hearts, we have to trust Him. It may not make sense, but it will always be worth it in the end. The same instruction from God that told me to go to Morehouse when I had never heard of the school was the same sense I felt to abruptly move to LA. The same inclination that told me to talk to Corbin in my freshman year was the same inclination that was telling me to change my flight. Call it the universe, instinct, or whatever makes sense, I know that the instruction out of nowhere to fly to LA was nothing but the voice of God, so I trusted it and changed my flight. "In order to be BALLIN', you have to B-ALL-IN."

Monday, August 19, was the day to leave Ohio for the ROSE 2019 Summit and then for Los Angeles. Arriving at the airport in Columbus, I was excited to see just how things were going to unfold. Luckily my family was 100 percent on board with me leaving Ohio, going to the summit, and then chasing my dream in LA.

It was sad to leave Tyson behind. His mother sent me a photo of him crying on the way home after they dropped me off. Change is always hard but a necessary part of growth.

When I arrived in Atlanta at approximately 1:00 p.m., I knew that what lay ahead would test me in ways that I had never imagined. The ROSE/ROBE team put me up in the Hyatt Regency Hotel for my stay during the summit. I had a stipend for food and Ubers. I also had my own hotel room. Those few days during the summit were some of the highlights of my summer. I had such a good time with my colleagues. The Bugg family sure knows how to have a good time. We had drinks at night after long days of working and even went to the Edgewood bars after the last day of workshops.

Throughout the summit I felt safe. Safe is not a feeling that I have often. As much as I am incredibly optimistic and hard-working, I very rarely feel safe because of money. I often feel like I am on edge because I never have enough funds to do what I need to, and that causes me to feel unsafe. During the summit, the Bugg family made sure that I had my hotel room, transportation, and food. They were fantastic hosts and made working at the summit a very pleasant experience.

Although the summit was going well, in the back of my mind I felt just a tad anxious because of my plans to jump over to Los Angeles. I kept telling myself to focus on the present moment and enjoy the fun while it lasted because LA was going to be challenging. By the last day of the summit, my stipend money had gotten low. It was then that reality hit me that the glorious support that came with working the summit was going to go away soon. No more Hyatt Regency, Ubers, and meals. As we packed up all the signage and props and said goodbye to guests, I was sad. I didn't want the summit to end; I was having such a good time. When I felt anxiety start to creep into my mind, I kept reminding myself to trust that everything would work out.

During the very last second of the summit, Dr. Kimari Bugg was saying goodbye to everyone and called me over. I was unsure what she wanted with me. I thought maybe she wanted me to carry something to her car. When I went over to her, she said, "Here you go, Chris! Thank you so much for helping out with the summit this year. We appreciate you!" As she said those words, she handed me a check for $550.

I gave her a big hug and almost started crying. I'm certain that she had no idea what I was going through or what my plans were, but that check meant more to me than she will ever know. That check meant oxygen for my dream. I was the crazy man who had a flight to LA in two days and only $25 in my pocket. The check gave me hope.

The summit ended at around 4:30 p.m. on a Friday, so I quickly ran to the bank and deposited that check in person. It was raining, and of course I had no car, so I ran. I ran from the summit to the nearest Bank of America I could find. Arriving at the bank, I was soaking wet, partly because of the rain, partly because of sweat. Luckily, I was able to get the check deposited and get out before the bank closed. I felt so relieved leaving that bank, smiling from ear to ear.

I still have the check she gave me and travel around with it often. That check represents to me what God can do when I trust Him. With the summit behind me and my check deposited, it was time to party and celebrate the completion of all of our hard work. Naturally, my two best friends, Corbin and Sean, came to the hotel and hung out with the ROSE/ROBE team too. Nothing makes me happier than when different people from different aspects of my life meet and have fun. Seeing Corbin talk with Wesley from the ROBE team and Sean talk to sisters from the Bugg family made my heart smile.

Corbin's birthday is August 25. We spent that weekend celebrating his birthday and having a good time with classmates. Between the summit, spending time with my friends, and turning up, that business trip to Atlanta was one of the best I ever had. Not once during the weekend did I inform my friends about my jump to LA. I kept partying with them as if nothing was going on. We partied all night long at a club in Buckhead called The Ivy. I remember arriving back at the hotel at 3:00 a.m. for a flight that was at 6:00 a.m. from Atlanta to Los Angeles. I went to The Ivy, back to my hotel, to the airport, to LA, all in the same sweaty outfit. #Yikes

Arriving in Los Angeles, I booked myself an Airbnb and stayed in Arlington Heights. I had two suitcases, $500, and trust that things were going to work out. I booked the Airbnb for a week because that was all I could afford. It was very rough. I had one top bunk bed in a room of eight other bunkbeds. The room was tight. I didn't know anyone, but it was what I called home for my first time back in Los Angeles.

I was super private about what I was experiencing during this time. I eventually told both Corbin and Sean about my living in a hostel in Los Angeles. Both of them were shocked. I was shocked myself that this had become my reality. Imagine being in a tight room filled with complete strangers, four sets of bunk beds, and no air conditioning. The room was infested with ants—I saw an entire trail of them going up the wall one morning—and of course the room reeked of marijuana. It was uncomfortable, but in my heart I felt I was doing what needed to be done to follow my vision. At this moment my faith was being tested.

One morning I woke up to an inch of toilet water on the room floor because the toilet was clogged and overflowed. Luckily, I had the top bunk, and I had left my luggage in the living room near the lockers. Everyone else was pissed to learn that toilet water had gotten on their belongings. I kept thinking, "This is going to make a great story for someone to read one day." My positive perspective and stoic behavior carried me through these moments.

After about a week of hell, I was granted an in-person interview at CAA. September 5 was the first time I had ever walked into the beautiful Century City building. I met with two gentlemen, Wilzon and Joe, who oddly enough were wearing NFL jerseys but were very kind. Walking into my interview, I wasn't nervous at all. I knew that I was meant to be at CAA, that the interview was going to go well, and that they were going to offer me a position. My faith was in the sign that I saw at the library weeks prior. I had trusted my instinct to make it this far and knew things would work out.

Almost a year after finishing graduate school and living in Atlanta and Ohio, I finally had found my next step. On September 17, 2019, I received an offer letter to officially join CAA as a mailroom clerk. I trusted the vision for myself, did what I needed to do, and finally got the job that I knew was for me. I broke away from the comfortability of Ohio and from the idea that my first job needed to be on a television set. I took a risk and took a chance on myself. Oprah always says, "Struggle is there to show you who you are." I firmly believe that this entire experience to get me to CAA showed me who I am: I'm someone who can take losses and experience hardships but can stand up and keep fighting until I win.

The lesson to take away from this story is to take risks. So often we take the easy, comfortable route, but I'm here to show you what happens when you take a risk. Trust that life will give you exactly what you need when you need it. Trust that you know what is best for you at all times. Trust that although you may have a divine vision for yourself, executing that vision will not always be easy.

It was hard changing my flight to LA on a whim. I had a tough time when I got to LA and had to live in a room with a bunch of strangers and toilet water on the floor, but this is what doing the work can sometimes look like. It's tough, messy, challenging, and sometimes seems irrational, but you must keep going. It really is true that what doesn't kill you makes you stronger. I'm so grateful for my journey. I'm happy to say that I believed, pushed toward my goal, and got the job I desired. Next time you find yourself at a crossroads, take a risk, take a chance, make a change, and break away toward the life of your dreams.

CHAPTER 10
Lessons from
My Job Search

Success seems to be connected to action. Successful people keep moving. They make mistakes, but they never quit.

—J.W. Marriot

THROUGHOUT COLLEGE I was able to land some pretty impressive internships. By my sophomore year at Morehouse, I was interning for 20th Century FOX in Los Angeles. The next summer after that I interned at *The Tonight Show Starring Jimmy Fallon* and was a member of NBC's prestigious Fellowship Program. In graduate school I was part of a small minority of students who landed a paid internship when I worked for Legendary Entertainment in Scripted Development. Navigating all of those companies, I became a resource for younger students, helping them polish their résumés and get prepped for interviews. I've even created YouTube videos based on my job search advice, which were featured in *USA TODAY* and *BlackEnterprise.*

Unfortunately, after I finished college, I had a hard time landing a full-time job. It was approximately 280 days from finishing graduate school to securing my first gig.

During the search there were moments when I was hopeless, stressed out, and depressed. I felt like no one could relate to my struggles. I thought I was alone, but according to a Gallup poll, I wasn't.

Gallup finds that unemployed Americans are more than twice as likely as those with full-time jobs to say they currently have or are being treated for depression—12.4 percent vs. 5.6 percent, respectively. However, the depression rate among the long-term unemployed—which the Bureau of Labor Statistics defines as those who have been seeking work for twenty-seven weeks or more—jumps to 18.0 percent.

My experience with job search depression was dreadful. It wasn't until I increased my job-seeking efforts significantly and started gaining momentum that I felt my depression subside. In a *Forbes* article, education and business expert Susan Adams writes:

> Not only is finding a job in your own hands but so is your mental health, which is directly linked to your ability to push ahead with your job search. Though looking for a job can be one of the toughest tasks in life, especially when you're feeling down, it's incredibly important to soldier on.

In my process to soldier on, I learned new tips and tricks that I wish someone would have told me earlier in my full-time job search. I understand that job-search depression is a real thing and that it is difficult for young adults to find work. Whether it is your aspiration to work in entertainment, business, retail, or any type of full-time work, I feel that these stories, tips, and tricks can be useful and help you secure employment. The following pages are excerpts from my blog, which teaches my best job-seeking tips that I've learned along my professional journey.

IN-PERSON MEETINGS

While battling the peaks and valleys of my job search, I was incredibly candid on social media about my adventures. It became a daily ritual for me to post on my Instastory, update my 4,000 plus LinkedIn followers, and tweet endlessly. Through sharing my life via social media, I have made lots of friends and been able to meet up with some of these people in person. Of all the positive opportunities that social media has given me, there was one meeting in particular that was different and taught me a valuable lesson that we must discuss.

A gentleman reached out to me on Instagram expressing to me that he had been following me on social media for a while and wanted to do drinks. Contrary to what some may believe, I am incredibly selective with whom I decide to associate myself and spend time. I understand that the most valuable asset that any of us have is time, and I hate to waste mine. On one hand, I suspected that this meeting could lead to nothing. On the other hand, I've always been taught to "take the meeting because you never know where that person could go." Betraying my higher self, I agreed to meet with this gentleman for drinks.

We met at a spot in Hollywood. That afternoon I caught an Uber to the cafe, paid for my bill, and Ubered back home. Our drinks meeting cost me an hour of my time and $30. Throughout the lunch, this gentleman talked down to me. There was never a moment when I felt that he was genuinely listening to me or providing valuable advice. Not once did he ask to read any of my writing or review my résumé. We never discussed how we could help each other with goals, nor did we trade contacts of people who might be beneficial. Listening to him talk was like listening to a bad high school graduation speech. When the bill came, I handed over my debit card, quickly called my Uber, and regretted that I had taken the meeting because I felt I had wasted my time and money.

Meeting people and networking are two ways to ensure success. There is a quote that says, "If you want to go fast, go alone. If you want to go far, go with others." This story is not to discourage taking drink dates altogether, but to try to do it effectively. That lunch meeting did not go well because I didn't ask myself the right questions beforehand. I don't ever want you to have that kind of experience. With that said, I would like to share five questions anyone should ask themselves before agreeing to meet with anyone from a cold message.

1. What Clear Goal Do I Have for This Meeting?

Whenever you decide to meet with someone you don't know well, you should have a clear and defined goal before taking the meeting. As soon as the gentleman reached out to me on Instagram and I agreed to meet with him, I should have come to the meeting with a clearly defined goal. I could have asked myself these questions:

- Do I need encouragement?
- Do I have a favor to ask?
- Am I interested in learning about this man's experience?
- What is my goal for this meeting?

None of us has time to waste. Not having a goal for the meeting meant I increased the risk of potentially wasting my time. One of my all-time favorite Bible verses is Proverbs 29:18, which says, "Where there is no vision, the people perish." I'd like to add to that by saying without vision, time will perish as well. Anytime you meet with anyone regarding a professional opportunity, you should have a vision of how you would like the meeting to go. Never agree to meet with a person without doing some real reflective work on what you think could potentially come out of the meeting. Do your homework, do some research, and approach every meeting with some substantial goals that will help move your career forward.

2. What Makes This Person Credible?

After you have goals for your meetings, the next question you should ask yourself every time is what is it that makes this particular individual you are meeting appropriate to assist you with your goal. Social media marketing is so easy. There are people out there who study the glitz and glamour of Instagram and duplicate what they see "successful" people doing to portray an image of how they want to be perceived. It is reasonably simple to be whoever you want to be online without doing actual work. It is always important to move through the world with keen skepticism to decrease the chance of being deceived. Ways to check for credibility would be to ask for work samples before the meeting, do substantial research on Google, or ask a friend for a second opinion on a person.

My field is the entertainment industry. Naturally if a person I'm meeting with is a television writer, I do my best to find credits on shows that this person may have earned. It is one thing to have on a LinkedIn or Twitter bio, *TV writer*. It is another thing to have a list of credits for shows on IMDB. No matter how private a person is or how loud their social media presence, work always speaks for itself. Whenever an individual does great work, someone will post about it or it will be available on a credible website. The internet is such a valuable asset and makes it incredibly easy to vet folks prior to a meeting. Before meeting with anyone, first check LinkedIn, then Twitter, then Google. Doing so will give you a glimpse into the type of person you are meeting with and what their background is.

3. Do We Have Any Mutual Friends?

Very rarely will a person have no social media presence, but if this is the case, I would say look for mutual friends. My best meetings have been those that have been through referrals. Mutual friends are an exquisite filter for weeding out people who could potentially waste your time. Your friends should know your taste, aspirations, and interests. If a person were to reach out to me stating that they have talked to one of my friends whom I trust first, I would be way more likely to want to meet with them. You can also ask your mutual friend about the person you are meeting with.

I have a classmate named JD who graduated with me from Morehouse. JD is an intelligent, hardworking brother whom I've grown to respect over the years. One day, JD hit me up to tell me that he was mentoring a college student named Laron. JD was well aware of my professional accolades and aspirations; he felt that Laron could benefit from a conversation with me. When JD reached out to me to speak to Laron, it was a no-brainer because JD was a person whom I had known and respected.

After JD introduced Laron and me via email, I was able to talk with Laron, and it was an incredible experience. Laron was sharp and asked insightful questions and fortunately I had answers. The exchange was positive and productive. These are the kinds of interactions I look for when networking. I would have been a lot more skeptical to meet with Laron had he reached out to me without JD's introduction. Having a mutual friend drastically increases the chances for a positive interaction.

4. Can I Afford to Entertain The Meeting?

Money is never something to play with. If you can't afford to get to the function and pay for yourself and potentially for your guest for a meeting, don't go. Like the popular Fergie song "Glamorous" says, "If you ain't got no money, take yo' broke ass home." I would like to add, "If you ain't got no money, *keep* yo' broke ass home."

There have been moments where I foot the bill of a person whose brain I was picking in an attempt to add some value to the interaction. I have had even more moments when a meeting will go so well that a person will pay for me. It happens. I appreciate moments when I am treated to a meal or drink, but I don't expect it. The last thing you want to be to anyone is a financial burden in the early stages of your relationship. If you can't afford your way at any given moment, stay home.

5. Would A Call Be More Beneficial?

Not everyone deserves an in-person meeting. Those meetings take time, energy, and resources. Sometimes it may be better to chat on the phone first to get more clarity and get a feel for a person. One rule of thumb I'm implementing for myself is to schedule a call early with people I don't know. I always want to meet new people, but if I or any of my friends are unfamiliar with who a person is, a call is an excellent place to start. On a call, I can ask the right questions, hear the sincerity in a person's voice, and get a better understanding of who they are before meeting in person.

COLD EMAILING

Cold emailing is a direct message between two people who have no prior contact with each other. Cold emailing is a difficult form of communication for two main reasons. One, it is expected that when you send a cold email, you have no relationship with the person you are attempting to connect with. Second, there is no non-verbal feedback that would enable you to change your approach in real-time. As a young professional, I have to cold email all the time.

Through hundreds of attempts to send cold emails successfully, I have found some helpful and actionable tips that I must share regarding cold emailing. If you implement these practices, I can say with confidence that doing so will greatly increase your responses to cold emails. With my methods, I have had informational interviews with executives, had my work reviewed by agents in Los Angeles, and have created great relationships in HR at entertainment companies. Trust me, cold emailing works if you work it. When crafting cold emails, LinkedIn InMails, or even Instagram DMS, your message should be able to answer three questions.

1. How Do You Know This Person?

An introduction sets the tone for the email and you want to start your message warmly by providing some context of how you met this person or where you know them from. This is a chance for you to show either you've done some impressive research on your target or you are connected to someone that they trust. Studies have shown that people are far more motivated to help others when they feel uniquely qualified to do so.

What This Looks Like:

Hello Nick, my name is Chris Sumlin. I recently met your friend Sean at an event in Atlanta, and we talked about how I was looking to find an internship in the media field this summer. He told me about your impressive work with 11Alive. After reviewing your LinkedIn profile, I would love for us to chat about your professional journey and experiences.

This opener instantly articulates two big points. The first is that this person is connected to someone I know. The second is I have done some research by checking out their profile. A message sent with this kind of clarity and personalization is effective.

2. How Can This Person Help Me?

It is important that you are clear about what your target can do for you and what that looks like. I have received cold messages that make me interested in helping the sender, but often the message doesn't give me a clear, actionable plan of what that help looks like. There have been moments when an individual messages me and asks for "help getting internships." My next question is usually, "Well, what does this help look like?" Is it a consultation phone call? Is it reviewing your résumé? Is it Skyping and doing a mock interview?

In her book *Dare to Lead,* Brené Brown says, "Clear is kind, unclear is unkind." She continues, "Feeding people half-truths or bullshit to make them feel better (which is almost always about making ourselves feel more comfortable) is unkind."

When you want help from someone, aim to be clear—go for it, and clearly ask for what you want. Doing so saves time and is respectful.

What This Looks Like:
One area I need to improve on is my interviewing skills. Would you be interested in a ten-minute Skype call sometime this week when I could practice interviewing with you? Let me know times you are available.

This approach is clear, bold, and provides a direct plan of how this person can help in the given situation.

3. Was I Considerate and Respectful?

After you explain who you are and how you can be helped, end with a sweet note. It is true that your target might be busy, but in my experience, people love to help whomever they can. Make sure you try to end with a nice note that acknowledges how busy your target is and how you appreciate the time to even read your message in the first place.

What This Looks Like:

I understand that you are busy, and I appreciate the time you took to read my message. I hope to hear from you soon and that you have a good rest of your week.

This wrap-up is warm, considerate, and respectful. It's also not too pushy or over the top.

Altogether this is how your message should read:

Hello Nick!

My name is Chris Sumlin. I recently met your friend Sean at an event in Atlanta, and we talked about how I was looking for an internship in the media field this summer.

He told me about your impressive work with 11Alive. After reviewing your LinkedIn profile, I would love for us to chat about your professional journey and get feedback on my job search.

One area I need to improve is my interviewing skills. Would you be interested in a ten-minute Skype call sometime this week when I could practice interviewing with you? Let me know times you are available.

I understand that you are busy, and I appreciate the time you took to read my message.

I hope to hear from you soon and that you have a good rest of your week.

Warm regards,

Chris Sumlin

- That message is fewer than 150 words.
- It sets a clear tone with a name drop.
- It establishes how the target can be helpful.
- It articulates humility and gratitude.

Cold emailing is similar to making new friends. Everyone is different and has their preferences, but there are some non-negotiables that make the process a tad easier. Always remember to do your best to be informed, clear, and humble. Don't be afraid to reach out to people and take a chance because you never know where it can take you.

THE IMPORTANCE OF RELATIONSHIPS

Throughout graduate school, I was encouraged to work at a talent agency to get my start in entertainment. The big three talent agencies are William Morris/Endeavor (WME), Creative Artists Agency (CAA), and International Creative Management (ICM). When I learned that these three agencies were the most popular, I focused all my efforts on trying to gain connections at these companies.

On August 6, 2019, I found the LinkedIn profile of an HR executive at WME. This man had a friendly profile picture and a summary that stated he had over eight years' experience in human resources. Upon viewing his profile, I assumed that if anyone could help me break into the doors at WME, it would be this gentleman. I sent him a LinkedIn request to connect, and within minutes he accepted my request. After the connection was made, I knew it was important that I message him quickly stating my intentions and how I hoped he could assist. My message read:

> Thank you for accepting my request… I hope to join [your company] one day… Do you know of anyone I can send my résumé to?

My message seemed direct, friendly, and respectful; making meaningful connections and asking for help is what LinkedIn was made for, right?

After sending the message, I thought perhaps I had overestimated my cold messaging skills because the HR executive never responded. Instead, eight days later a HR coordinator from the same company reached out stating that the HR executive I had contacted had passed my résumé over to him. Mind you, this was news to me because my question to the HR executive was never answered.

The next day the HR coordinator and I hopped on the phone for an introductory call in which I shared my career goals with him. Our call was fantastic, and during our conversation, I learned about the business model of WME and was invited to come in for an in-person interview.

When I met in-person the friendly gentleman with whom I'd had a phone call, it was a pleasant experience. I walked into the building, shook his hand, and followed him into his office. When I sat down he told me, "You know, Chris, I've reviewed your résumé before. I found you on LinkedIn a while back and was considering you for a position, but the executive I was recruiting for went in a different direction. We are familiar with your work and experiences."

Our meeting was positive, and I appreciated my time at WME that day. Unfortunately, I was told during the meeting that the company wasn't looking to fill any entry-level roles that day, but that they would for sure be in touch. This entire experience taught me some valuable lessons that I must share with you.

Before I even reached out to the executive in HR at WME, the HR coordinator already knew of my résumé. There's a quote that I often see on Instagram that states, "Your name is in rooms that your feet haven't touched yet." I always read that quote and thought it was cool but never really believed it. When the HR coordinator told me he knew of me, had already seen my résumé, and even considered me for a position before I ever reached out, the quote became real for me.

I walked away from that meeting inspired and encouraged. Stoic philosophy teaches there are only two types of things in life: things we can control and things we cannot control. It is our job to do our best work and put it out into the world; that is all we can control. What we can't control is who sees it, how it makes them feel, or the impact we have had on others. Never be ashamed to tell people who you are and what it is that you do. People love to talk about other people, especially those wild enough to believe in the magic of their dreams. Put yourself out there in any way that you can because you never know the impact it may have on a person or the opportunity it can manifest for you.

It is also important to acknowledge how a relationship with a person can be more influential than a stand-alone résumé. The HR coordinator at WME already knew of my résumé, but it wasn't until I sent the cold message to one of his colleagues that I was afforded a meeting. It is important that in moments of job seeking, we all continue to make relationships if we want to earn amazing opportunities. You, just like me, may have an impressive résumé, but relationships are just as important, if not more important, to make sure that someone sees that résumé. Big lesson.

Advocacy is also one of the most powerful factors in a job search. I know that my résumé is much more impactful in an applicant pool when someone on the inside advocates for it. Making allies and friends on the inside can move your career forward.

With any aspect of life, there are always peaks and valleys, and a job search is no different. Whether you are going after your first job or are unemployed looking for a new job, remember these gems. Do your best to be patient with yourself and do the best you can as you seek employment.

CHAPTER 11
Dealing with Being Disliked

The weight of one's opinion of you is as heavy as you allow it to be.

–Unknown

LIVING AND WORKING in Los Angeles was a daunting experience. It's one thing to be an intern and work in LA for a semester or summer. It is a completely different experience working full time with no plans of leaving anytime soon. It was October 7, 2019, when this became my reality. At the time I was twenty-five. Being on my own forced me to be responsible for how I spent my time, money, and managed my well-being. There was no one coming to do my laundry, no one coming to feed me or make sure I got to work on time. I felt like the growth that I experienced during my first couple months in Los Angeles was unlike any other period of my life. In this period of growth, I learned how to have my own back and be my own man.

In addition to working a new job, I moved into a new house in Hollywood with a bunch of roommates. Whether at work or at home, I was constantly on guard as I was meeting new people wherever I went. Nothing around me felt familiar or comfortable. Meeting new people is quite an experience because you never truly know who has your back or whom you can trust. In the South, when I lived in Atlanta, I had the enormous support of my friends and family-like folk from the Morehouse community, and that took time to build. Back home in Ohio, things felt familiar because Ohio is where I grew up and where my parents live. The West Coast was much different. In Los Angeles, everyone is working toward something and trying to network their way to the top. In my experience, LA is all about who you know and how you can help others get to their goals.

Riding in Ubers around LA, I frequently was asked, "What do you do?" Going to parties in Hollywood, it was always, "Where do you work?" I didn't like that at all because I felt no one cared about me as a person. Some people in Los Angeles were connected, talented, and good-looking but total jerks. There were other people I met who may not have necessarily been all of those things but were still a joy to be around. I wanted to be a mix of both. I aimed to be a person of value and a man of humility.

Each day, I did my best to keep my ego in check. I didn't want to be the guy sitting around thinking about where I worked or the degrees I had earned. I did my best to meet people just where they were, looking past their accolades. What I learned was that when you meet people with love and empathy regardless of their job title or socio-economic background, that is how you make an authentic connection.

With that in mind, I simply did my best to be incredibly candid and loving toward those I encountered. I expected that if I showed up with love and humility that I would receive that same energy in return. At work and with my roommates, I was a guy known for cracking jokes, laughing loudly, and talking to anyone who would listen. Most of the time my socializing methods and fun personality worked, which made me feel good.

Unfortunately, there were times when my personality didn't work, and I rubbed people the wrong way. There were moments when I would accidentally offend people or piss them off and they ended up not liking me. Whenever these moments were brought to my attention, I did my best to try to remedy the situation. What I've come to learn is that sometimes we all will have to deal with being disliked no matter who we are.

Dr. Martin Luther King Jr. is one of the most iconic figures in African American History. As a social activist, Morehouse College graduate, and Baptist minister, Dr. King played a vital role in shaping African American civil rights in the 1950s and 1960s. Through his speeches and sermons, King advocated for peace and equality. His efforts and legacy are still remembered and honored to this day. Since King's death in 1968, *US News and World Report* states, at least 955 streets in the United States have been named after King. While many today consider Dr. King to be an iconic hero, an early 1968 Harris Poll found that King had a public disapproval rating of nearly 75 percent. In the last years of his life, even King dealt with disapproval and being disliked.

Being disliked is no fun. I know I hate it. I believe wholeheartedly that we humans are hardwired for connection. When evaluating the evolution of mammals from small rodents to humans, studies have shown that we are profoundly shaped by our social environment and that "we suffer greatly when our social bonds are threatened or severed." No one wants to be alone or disliked. The Bible states in Genesis 2:18, "It is not good for man to be alone." The need to have friends and family and be a part of communities is at the core of who we are.

As much as we are hardwired for connection and community, it can be tough to achieve, and sometimes we may piss people off in the process. So how do we manage that? How do we accept someone's disapproval or their dislike of us? Some might argue we should not care what people think at all; that's one option.

Trying to balance the innate desire to have community while not caring what people think is difficult. Think about the last time you started a new job, attended a conference, or were at a party where you didn't know many people. It's common to observe those around us and self-assess, wondering if we can fit in. Self-assessment is healthy, but sometimes it's easy to fall into a rabbit hole of measuring ourselves and self-worth according to others' standards of what we should be. This is how social phobia starts. The Anxiety and Depression Association of America defines social phobia as "intense anxiety or fear of being judged, negatively evaluated, or rejected in a social or performance situation."

I went to a mixer once in LA and was trembling as I walked into the function. I wondered, *Will people like me? Will I be accepted?* As I stood around, letting these questions ruminate in my mind, I was paralyzed with fear. In moments of self-doubt and uncertainty, what is the underlying problem? I began to ask myself how I could be so confident in certain moments and utterly vulnerable and lost in others. For me, it boils down to prioritizing what others think of me and being afraid of being disliked.

I do think we all have moments when it is easier to be ourselves in certain situations more so than in others. When I am with my family or friends, I feel minimal judgment. In those settings I'm not concerned with being disliked because I've found people who love and accept me. Unfortunately, that is not always going to be the case, and there are times where I will be in new environments such as when I first moved to LA. In moments of extreme social anxiety, it is crucial to allow these moments to occur, assess them, and find ways of managing ourselves better. Oprah said it best: "Your life journey is about learning to become more of who you are and fulfilling the highest, truest expression of yourself as a human being. That's why [we're all] here." The only way we can get on this journey of truly being ourselves is to stop worrying about what others think of us, be okay with being disliked, and live life boldly.

One weekend while living in Los Angeles, I went to a club called Arena KTown, located in the Koreatown neighborhood. Prior to going to Arena, I made sure I had a couple slider sandwiches from Subway and lots of water. The club is rather small and gets packed quickly. I naturally sweat a lot, so before going to Arena I always make sure to hydrate and prepare for what I know is going to be a lit night. Most nights I go out with friends, but this night I was alone and went to the club by myself. I knew that I would have fun either way and that I would be safe; no one in Koreatown was going to cause me any harm. As I walked into the club, the music was bumping, the crowd was lit, and everyone was dancing their hearts out. I vividly remember taking a video of the club to post on Instagram and captioning it, "It's 11:30 and the club is jumpin' jumpin.'"

I was lit and having a good time. In the midst of the turn up, everyone in the club formed a circle. The circle allowed anyone who was brave enough to be the center of attention and dance. The DJ was playing the hits. People were drinking, dancing, and having a ball. When the DJ played

"Be Faithful" by Fatman Scoop, a young woman jumped into the middle of the circle and danced her heart out. She had thick, curly brown hair, and she was wearing a jumpsuit and hoop earrings. Watching her dance from the wall, I really wanted to dance. Seeing her not care whether anyone liked her or not made me want to do the same. Unfortunately, I didn't. During the night I just stood there on the wall with my phone in hand recording rather than dancing. I was too concerned about embarrassing myself or being judged.

Following that moment at the club, I desired to be more authentic. I wanted to be like that woman at the club. I wanted to be free. I decided that night that I would no longer let social anxiety get the best of me. I was going to be my most authentic self at all times and learn to be okay if someone didn't like it. This energy followed me at work. When I got to the office that Monday, I increased my socializing at work even more. If I wanted to smile, I smiled. If I wanted to say hello, I did. It was my intention to be a force of positivity, fun and authenticity. I have to give myself credit; some moments I felt my efforts were successful. I began to text my coworkers and make friends, and this gave me confidence to keep up my momentum. But, of course, I didn't win everyone.

There was one person in particular who was not a fan of my "in-your-face" personality and joking candor. The weekend after my efforts to be a "strong force of positivity" in the office, it was brought to my attention that one of my coworkers shared with a group of people that she didn't like me. Luckily one of my friends was there and happened to hear the interaction. After eavesdropping on the conversation, my friend told me how one of the assistants at work stated to a group of colleagues, "He rubs a lot of people the wrong way. I'm not a fan and don't like him at all."

Allegedly this assistant then went on to give examples of moments where I was "reckless" or less than considerate of others. After hearing the negative impact I'd had on some of my coworkers, I was hurt and shocked. This moment triggered the social anxiety I thought I had conquered. Naturally, I started beating myself up, overthinking, and feeling insecure. My feelings came partly because someone didn't like me and partly because the situation caught me off guard. I couldn't even fathom someone disliking me, especially at work. This was the first time I had ever experienced work gossip and being disliked in a professional setting.

After that negative report from my friend about a coworker not liking me, I had to figure out how I was going to manage the situation. I've come up with four lessons that have helped me battle social anxiety and manage being disliked.

OPINION VS. EXPERIENCE

The first step in dealing with being disliked is to evaluate whether the person disliking you is sharing a meaningless opinion or valid experience. So often when people share negative thoughts about us, we have a propensity to say things like, "Well that's your opinion." Disregarding a person's thoughts as an opinion isn't necessarily productive and shouldn't be our first step. As much as we may not like it, maybe the person is sharing their valid experience, and if they are, we must listen. There is a difference between someone's wonky opinion and their lived experience.

Let's say for example I go to a restaurant and my waiter is a young man named Stryker. Unbeknownst to me, Stryker is very kind. He takes his grandmother grocery shopping, has an adorable puppy that he takes for walks, and is really involved in his church. Everyone in the community loves Stryker. However, the Stryker I experience is much different. On the night I come into the restaurant, Stryker is overworked and going through stuff at home. He's been working a double shift, his girlfriend just dumped him, and he's not being his usual friendly self. The Stryker I experience is not the kind gentleman who walks his dog and takes his grandmother to the grocery store. I experience Stryker as disengaged, short-fused, and rude.

If I walk out of that restaurant and tell myself, "That waiter Stryker is a rude person. I don't like him and will make sure he never serves me again," that sentiment wouldn't just be an opinion but my experience. I didn't know that Stryker is a nice guy who does all these great things in his community. I only experienced Stryker as rude and short-fused. People only know what they know. Everyone is valid in their experiences. When someone shares their experience and their experience causes us to be disliked, it is vital that we acknowledge our part in it.

When this coworker of mine explained how I "rub a lot of people the wrong way," instead of just disregarding her statement as a mere opinion, I had to entertain the possibility that me rubbing people the wrong way was her experience. After coming to this awareness, first I had to forgive myself for possibly rubbing people the wrong way. Second, I had to forgive her for sharing her experience with others. Third, I had to make a concerted effort to make sure that I behaved more appropriately. Once I was able to take a breath and implement these steps, I felt better following the situation.

This practical approach takes emotional maturity and practice to develop. This thinking prevented me from taking it personally that this woman had a negative experience of me. I was able to use that opportunity to grow and better manage being disliked.

SELF-REFLECTION AND MEDITATION

Being disliked at work also taught me the importance of self-reflection and meditation. Self-reflection—also called introspection—is the practice of observing and analyzing oneself to grow as a person. When I was informed that I was rubbing people the wrong way, I could have handled that situation poorly. I could have gone up to that assistant, cussed her out, and told her she was lying, intensifying the situation. Instead I went home and meditated on my behavior and looked for ways to improve.

Meditation has a multitude of benefits. Each day I try to spend at least 30 minutes a day in silence, unplugged, and evaluate my thoughts. *Insider* reports, "The mental health benefits of meditation include better focus and concentration, improved self-awareness and self-esteem, lower levels of stress and anxiety, and fostering kindness." Spending time focusing on your thoughts, self-reflection, and breathing are something I would recommend.

Being self-reflective is also a way to craft your own identity. I believe that it is far easier to be offended by people's experiences and opinions when you don't take time to get to know yourself. When you know you are and actively work at being a better person, you become powerful.

I think if you were to ask anyone who the strongest animal in the jungle is, many would say a lion. Lions are fierce, strong, and reportedly 7 1/2 times stronger than a human. But at circuses all over the country, lions are put on display as entertainment and controlled by lion tamers with sticks. Imagine being a lion, 7 1/2 times stronger than a human, and having a man with a stick tell you what to do. The only way a lion can be controlled by a lion tamer is because the lion has been trained to forget who it is. No lion who understood the enormity of its own strength would be controlled by a stick. When we let someone's off-the-cuff comment control us and offend us, we are displaying the same idiotic behavior as a circus lion. We have to remember who we are at all times and do our best to exhibit strength. A way to find that strength is to find who we are through self-reflection.

I encourage anyone who gets embarrassed easily or is easily offended to do more introspective work. In the world of social media, friends, and lots of other stimulating activities, it can be hard to take time out of your day to get still and be self-reflective. Regardless of how difficult it may be, self-reflective work is essential to finding who you are. The power you will receive from meditation and self-reflection will assist you in fully standing in your essence. Being able to stand in your power makes it incredibly more difficult for someone to throw you off base by disliking you, because you are standing on a solid foundation of self-identity.

APOLOGIZING

Back at home, I had another instance of being disliked by one of my roommates. One evening at the house, everyone was vibing in the kitchen and getting along. I was in the kitchen cooking a meal, and one of my roommates brought home two bottles of wine. After everyone had a few glasses of wine, we ended up debating politics. I can say from experience that two things that should never mix are politics and wine.

One of my roommates was on the conservative side of the political spectrum, advocating for less in taxes and less government regulation. As she explained her argument, I continued to respond to every claim she made with counterarguments. It would be one thing if I just had stuck to my arguments and facts, but instead I hit below the belt and called my roommate an idiot. We went from healthy debate of opposing points of view to personal attacks about each other.

The next morning before she left for work, I got a phone call that was very unpleasant. My roommate expressed to me that she had felt incredibly disrespected and that I had been out of line. She later expressed to another housemate that she did not like me, and she felt I was an arrogant know-it-all. We didn't talk for weeks until she finally confronted me about how she felt about the entire situation in a calmer manner. When she humbly explained how she felt disrespected, I apologized.

In this experience of my roommate not liking me, I had to hear her experience, self-reflect on where I went wrong, and apologize for my poor behavior. Whenever we find ourselves at odds with other people, sometimes the best solution is to apologize for our part in the disagreement. Giving a heartfelt apology can be a powerful step to remedy someone's dislike of us.

DEVELOPING THICK SKIN

Dealing with being disliked is hard. There are moments when our efforts to establish relationships and make friends fail. When someone doesn't like us, we can evaluate their experience, be self-reflective, and apologize when we need to. Those are three helpful tips when experiencing dislike at work, at home, or in day-to-day life. But what about haters? How do we deal with disapproval from people who don't mean anything to us? These individuals can be former classmates, exes, toxic family members, or social media bots. The way we deal with being disliked from these kinds of people is through developing thick skin.

Clinical psychologist and professor in Pasadena, California, Dr. Ryan Howes, says, "If you've had skin ripped away [because of] trauma, or never developed thicker skin [because you were] sheltered from adversity, you'll experience every bump and sharp point with excruciating precision."

There are fewer and fewer people talking about developing thick skin. Because of social media and isolation, many people today live in echo chambers. The Goodwill Community Foundation defines an echo chamber as "an environment where a person only encounters information or opinions that reflect and reinforce their own." Sometimes we aren't going to be in echo chambers, and we are going to be met with harsh criticism and will need thick skin to not let the criticism take us down.

First, it is important not to take things personally. When a person in whom you have no investment harshly criticizes you, it's likely that the person's feedback is more about them than about you. Life can be competitive. There can be a time when someone sees you winning, and it ignites the insecurities in them. When you feel that a person is just being a low-life, don't engage or take it personally.

Another way to develop thick skin is to fight back. Contrary to my first point, sometimes you do, in fact, have to let people know what time it is. Don't let a person's criticism bully you into living small. Stick to your values and advocate for yourself when you need to. The more you stand up for yourself, the better you will get at it. Confrontation doesn't always mean getting low down and dirty, but you can fight back respectfully while keeping calm.

Third, accept the inevitable that not everyone will like you. We cannot live off the validation, approval, or approbation of others no matter how good it may feel. I would be a fool to think that everyone is going to like me, think I'm funny, or enjoy my books. That is not real life. When I walk into a room with my big personality, big ambitions, and loud laugh, it is going to rub some people the wrong way. That is the fact that I learned to accept. I have also learned that for every person who doesn't like me, there are ten who do. What I have come to understand is how important it is to have people around you who just love you for you. Everyone needs a tribe. I can say with confidence that you may not be for everyone, but you are definitely for someone.

Life is a journey, and one way to make life easier is not to get caught in the trap of caring what others think and to be okay with being disliked. These tips are ones that I'm still struggling to implement daily—it's tough. I'm hoping that after reading this story, you feel more empowered to break free from the prison of worrying about what other people think. Assess yourself, take these tips in, and do your best to take action. Being confident and being free serves us all more than being insecure and bound. Once you start doing the real legwork of loving yourself and standing firm in who you are, someone can say to you, "I don't like you," and you can respond with, "So what?"

CHAPTER 12
The Birthday Goodbye

If you are not willing to risk the unusual,
you will have to settle for the ordinary.
                                        –Jim Rohn

WORKING AT Creative Artists Agency was the ride of a lifetime. I enjoyed working there, met lots of great people, and was grateful for the experience. The talent agency world is a very distinct one. I had never experienced anything like it. I have nothing but respect for anyone who works in that space because anyone who works at a talent agency from the top down works incredibly hard. Being in the CAA building, I got first-hand experience in how the entertainment world truly works. In the mailroom, I met lots of fantastic people whom I know will be lifelong friends.

During the holiday season, things were very busy. As a mailroom clerk I was running around making sure that gifts, mail, and packages were being delivered efficiently. All of us who were in the building at the time were working very hard. When it came time for our two-week winter break, I had time to breathe and self-reflect. In the midst of my time away from the office, I started doing more writing. I was able to look back and see what I had done on my own without the backing of a company. Before I got to CAA, I was free to do whatever I wanted to do and be whoever I wanted to be. When I was in orientation to start my job at CAA, it became clear that I was a part of a company much bigger than myself, and that this came with sacrifices.

As an employee I had to be loyal to my company and follow their standards. We worked ten-hour days, Monday through Friday. The social media presence I had built throughout college took a major hit. I was expected to wear suits every day of the week and exude professionalism at all times. During winter break when I finally had time to clear my head and reflect on my past, I realized I missed my old life.

I missed when I was just Chris Sumlin and was able to do whatever it was that I desired. I didn't have to worry about a tweet offending someone at my company and embarrassing them. When you sign up to work for any company you do so understanding that everything you do is not just a reflection of you but your place of employment as well. Your actions, social media posts, and presence represent your company.

I understood the enormity of CAA and all that it was. CAA is considered one of the most influential agencies in Hollywood. The client list and the work that CAA does speaks for itself. Working there is no small deal at all. It is very common for anyone who graduates from college aspiring to work in the entertainment field to want work there first. I knew that it was a privilege that I worked at such a prestigious company.

Conversely, I began talking to my friends about why I felt I wasn't a good fit for the agency world. The company is not bad by any means. It just wasn't where I could see myself long-term. The few short months I was at the agency felt like a lifetime. I had grown so much from the day I walked in for an interview in September 2019 until January 2020. When I first stepped into the building, I was battling home-lessness and had no clothes. I was adjusting to the new city and trying to figure out who I was in this new chapter of my life. Once things settled and I had gotten into the routine of corporate work life, I felt like I was losing myself. Some-where inside I felt that maybe it was time to leave.

I started praying and asking God for some direction. As a new person to LA, I had started attending OASIS LA, a church located in Koreatown. The pastor there, Pastor Ju-lian, taught me so much about trusting God. By the winter of 2019, I had become a regular member of the church and decided to get baptized in the church that December. Being baptized, I felt like I was getting a fresh start. I felt like any mistake I had made or sin I had engaged in was washed away. Winter break allowed me to come back to myself, get closer to God, and get some direction. On January 5, 2020, I felt in my heart that it was time to make a change, and that change was quitting my prestigious agency job at CAA. One truth that I always hold is that there never is a right time to make a big decision. The biggest decisions in life happen by action, not by waiting around for anyone to validate what you know in your heart to do. I woke up that Sunday morning knowing what I wanted to do. I was ready to quit my job.

Winter break was so refreshing. It felt so good, and I had no interest in going back to work and working the long 9:00 a.m. to 7:00 p.m. days that my job required of me. I was tired of catching the bus from Hollywood to Century City. It was exhausting wearing suits every day and paying for dry cleaning every two weeks because I had limited clothes. When I logically weighed the pros and cons, I couldn't see how working at an agency could keep me inspired. I couldn't reconcile my reality and keep showing up to work knowing that I was unhappy. Life is too short. While I was at work, I would daydream about writing television scripts and more books. I was constantly envisioning myself going to schools and inspiring students. I wanted to create content and be free. I couldn't do my own thing while being under the umbrella of CAA. Doing so would be duplicitous and lack integrity.

Before going to church that morning I said, "God, if it is for me to leave my job, give me a sign during church service today."

Walking into the church sanctuary I was ready for my sign. I wasn't sure how it was going to come, but I trusted that God would show up for me. As God would have it, Pastor Julian Lowe preached a sermon entitled, "Learning to Live the Lifestyle of Jesus." The message was incredibly powerful and moving. Of all the things that Pastor Julian could have preached about, he just happened to preach about living on faith and on purpose.

One of the scriptures presented in Pastor Julian's sermon was John 15:7, which reads, "If you remain in me and my words remain in you, ask whatever you wish, and it will be done for you." (New Living Translation) Following that scripture, Pastor Julian discussed how important it is to improve the quality of our prayers. When he said that I was struck because I knew that I had been praying not for a "new job" but for direction to live out God's purpose in my life. I felt that he was talking to me throughout the entire sermon.

One example he used really struck me. Pastor Julian told the story of Adam and Eve and how in the Bible God told them to "be fruitful and multiply," but the serpent told them to consume the fruit that they were supposed to use as seeds. He illustrated his point by saying, "God said, 'Be fruitful.' The enemy said, 'Eat fruit.' So the enemy made them consume what they were supposed to be."

When he said those words, I thought about how I was a part of the agency world and helping the staff support the Hollywood stars. I reflected on how maybe I was consuming content instead of moving in the direction of creating it.

The statement that Pastor Julian made next brought it home for me: "Why do you think we have such a consumer culture? Because the enemy knows you will binge-watch Netflix for eight hours, and you're supposed to be a writer. So you will consume what God called you to be."

I knew that God was speaking through him. I had never met Pastor Julian. I hadn't expressed to him who I was or that I aspired to work in entertainment. He didn't even know who I was or that I was there. The fact that he used this particular example gave me the sign that I needed that it was time to leave the agency world and get back to my dream of creating content and writing. Sitting in the balcony, tears began to form in my eyes.

Right after that statement, Pastor Julian then said, "Balcony do you hear what I said? You better get off Netflix. There might be a creative gift on your life."

I wish I could make this story up, but it all was so timely and perfect. That was the statement for me that was the final straw. At that very moment I knew that I was going to quit my job. In college I had made it very clear that I desired to write and create content. Early on it became clear to me that the agency world isn't for writers. Agencies represent the writers; writers actually write.

Commuting on the bus in Hollywood to Century City and working 9:00 a.m. to 7:00 p.m. disallowed me to have time to create anything. There were days when I would leave my home as the sun was coming up and would leave the office when the sun was down. I didn't have time to work on my scripts like I desired. I chugged out a few blogs here and there, but I wasn't giving my craft the time needed to actually be good at what I was trying to do. It was also tough walking up the street in the suits, headed toward the Avenue of the Stars day in and day out.

There had come a moment where I was so immersed in the agency world that I forgot my dream. Between the break that I got in winter break and hearing Pastor Julian's sermon, I knew it was time for me to leave the agency world and get back to chasing my dream of creating content. In the church parking lot I had the same feeling that I felt when I saw the CAA book in the library. It was the same feeling that told me to jump from Columbus to Los Angeles. It's this instinctual, affirming feeling that I can only describe as hearing the voice of God.

Once I felt that feeling, I knew that I needed to call my mother. My mom has done her best to support me in all my dreams and endeavors. If I could get my Mom's approval, then I knew that I would be ready to quit as soon as possible. My heart raced as my iPhone read, "Calling Mom." I wasn't sure how she would respond. I spoke to her in the same way that my dad did when he decided he wanted to start a church back in 1995. I told her that my quitting wasn't a decision I was battling with but a decision I had made and that I wanted her blessing. I told my mom how I knew how long I had wanted to get a job, and then when I finally got it I was ready to leave after just a few months. Graciously she agreed with me and stated how she felt that it was the right thing to do.

That was January 5; my birthday is January 7. It was my plan to go into work that Tuesday and formally quit my job as a dedication to myself for my twenty-sixth birthday.

The night before my birthday I prayed so hard that the next day I would have a good day. Being in LA away from my friends, having to go to work, and not having a lot of resources, the possibility for the day to go south was there. I prayed and asked God for a day of joy and peace. I prayed for the courage and strength that I would be able to quit my job with confidence and minimal nerves. Going to sleep that night I felt peace knowing that I had prayed my best and the rest was up to God.

On Tuesday, January 7, 2020, I woke up ready to take the day on like a champion. On this day I was officially *Halfway Thru My 20s* as I had just turned twenty-six. The challenges that lay ahead were evident. I needed to get to the gym for some morning cardio, get dressed for work, get to work and tell my boss that I was leaving to pursue my dream of creating content.

Once I got to work, I was bombarded with love from everyone wishing me a Happy Birthday. I expressed to my work best friend Kristi that I was leaving CAA to try my hand at working to create content and to chase my dreams. I told her how important it was that I began working on creating some fire writing samples and networking with television executives around Los Angeles. Kristi wasn't shocked at all. She looked at me and said, "I remember you telling me that you wouldn't be here long during our first week of orientation."

Kristi didn't lie. Working at CAA I had learned a lot about myself and the entertainment world, and I even made friends. It was a good run, but I knew it wasn't going to last long.

Mid-way through the day I called my supervisors aside. It was a full circle moment as these two gentlemen were the guys I interviewed with. I had no nerves but simply told them that I really liked working at CAA but felt that it wasn't for me. I expressed how I felt, that I was holding a spot for a young college graduate who may have truly wanted to be there and how I was wrong for occupying that spot. My supervisors gave me hugs and told me how proud they were of me for making that decision for myself. The love and support I felt from them reassured me that everything was going to be all right.

Walking out of our short meeting my boss Wilzon said, "I feel like I will see you around." I replied and said, "Oh I'll be back—as a client." We all laughed, and my resignation process officially began.

My twenty-sixth birthday was by far one of the best birthdays I had ever had. Two of my colleagues, Ashley and Brittani, brought me a birthday cake and took me out to lunch. That evening some of my colleagues and I hit The Crack Shack for drinks to celebrate my birthday. Many people also came to congratulate me on announcing my departure from the company. I went home that night with a heart full of joy as I was closing another chapter of my journey. I have no regrets about the choices I've made to get to this point. The biggest reason I decided to work at CAA in the first place was to meet people. When I think about some of the incredible people I met in those few months, I smile. Regardless of what happens, I know that some of the people I've met there will be my friends for life.

The biggest lesson to take away from this story is to leave situations that don't fulfill you. So often in life we accept circumstances that don't satisfy us because we feel it is all we can get. This thinking is rooted in fear and scarcity. I firmly believe that we live in an abundant universe filled with goodness and opportunities. I can unequivocally say that CAA is a great company. This is by no means to slander them. It was quite a ride and I enjoyed it so much. I probably could have stayed at CAA a little longer, but I knew I had reached a point where I wasn't taking it as seriously as I could have. I wasn't giving it my best and knew that I could do something different. I quit my job because it wasn't working for me, and I knew I could find something more suitable.

This story reminds me of Donald Glover who quit his job as a featured cast member of the NBC sitcom *Community*. Glover is a talented rapper, TV writer, and actor. When speculation began to rise about why Donald left a successful show like *Community*, he took to Instagram and wrote, "I didn't leave *Community* to rap. I don't wanna rap. I wanted to be on my own."

There's a freedom that comes with betting on yourself and leaving a situation for your own independence. While some predicted that maybe Donald Glover's career would be over, he has since gone on to create his own scripted television series and become the first Black man to win Outstanding Directing for a Comedy Series at the Emmys. We can only speculate what might have happened to Donald Glover if he had stayed on *Community* and not taken a chance on himself.

Actress, comedian, and talk show co-host Amanda Seales was a host on a popular daytime show called, *The Real*. After one season of working on the show, she announced that she would not continue on as a co-host on *The Real*, stating she did not renew her contract because of "a lack of Black voices at the top." It was later announced that same month that she would host the 2020 BET Awards. It is wild how when you step out on faith and bet on yourself, opportunities present themselves.

On January 31, 2020, I signed my third book deal just a short period after leaving my job at CAA. The very book you hold in your hand is a demonstration that life goes on after leaving an incredible opportunity. When you bet on yourself and live on your own accord, miraculous things can happen. Although everyone's path looks different, it is so crucial that you lead the life that you want regardless of how unorthodox it may look to others.

Life is too short to waste a single minute not living on purpose and for ourselves. Whatever we do we must do it with intention, with conviction, and with faith knowing that everything always works out in the end.

Be inspired!

Acknowledgments

First and foremost, I would like to thank God for giving me the thoughts, ideas, and passion to write this book. Thank you to everyone whose name was mentioned in this book. Thank you for your love, support, and wisdom.

Thank you to Emily Hitchcock, Brad Pauquette, Doug Davis, and the Boyle & Dalton team for making this book possible.

To my parents, Monica and ET, and my siblings, Orlando, William, and Britney: Thank you for being incredibly supportive and loving. I'm grateful for my living grandmothers, Linda and Tanya. Thank you to Kevin Griffie for being a fantastic friend since I was fourteen years old. I want to give a special shout-out to my Morehouse brothers and best friends: Corbin Sanders, Sean Sheppheard, John Eagan, Jamil Muhammad, and Russell Pointer, Jr. Thank you all for the brotherhood and support through the years.

To my mentors from afar: Marie Forleo, who reminds me that "Everything is Figureoutable." To Oprah Winfrey, who has continually taught me about spirituality and intention. To Barack Obama, who has taught me how to have grace and poise as a Black man. To Beyoncé, who has taught me the importance of work ethic and drive.

It's also great when people believe in your vision. With that said I'd love to give a special shout out to the following:

Shakira Campbell
Kristal Chilton
Derrick Coles
Jarita Core
Equel Easterling
Stacy Eastmond
Karen L. Forest
DeAnna Fowkles
Tiffany Gaymon
Richard Gibbs
Ayana Hart
Andre Jackson
Jazmin Jervis
Malik Johnson
Kahdijah Jones
Marvin McMillan II
Jamaal Ridley
Meko Smith
Mario Stephens II
Ryan Sullivan
Sam Walk
Shekinah Williams

To all of my incredible supervisors at the numerous companies mentioned throughout the book. To the great schools I had the honor of attending. And, finally, to my readers and supporters. The list goes on and on. Thank you for your kindness and generosity. Thank you for cheering me on and cheering me up. I hope you enjoyed reading about my experiences and that this book inspires you in powerful ways.

Bibliography

Ackerman, Courtney E. "What Is Self-Esteem? A Psychologist Explains." [2020 Update] positivepsychology.com. www.positivepsychology.com/self-esteem (accessed October 31, 2020).

"Beyoncé is Now a 24-Time Grammy Winner / Edges Closer to Tying All-Time Record Among Women." https://thatgrapejuice.net/2020/01/beyonce-now-24-time-grammy-winner-edges-closer-tying-time-record-among-women (accessed November 12, 2020).

Brown, Brené. *Dare to Lead: Brave Work, Tough Conversations, Whole Hearts.* New York: Random House Large Print Publishing, 2019.

Centers for Disease Control and Prevention. Alcohol Related Disease Impact (ARDI) application, 2019. Available at www.cdc.gov/ARDI.

Cobb, James C. "When Martin Luther King Jr. Was Killed, He Was Less Popular than Donald Trump Is Today." *USA Today*, Gannett Satellite Information Network. April 5, 2008. www.usatoday.com/story/opinion/2018/04/04/

martin-luther-king-jr-50-years-assassination-donald-
trump-disapproval-column/482242002/.

Cook, Gareth. "Why We Are Wired to Connect." Scientific
American. October 22, 2013. www.scientificamerican.com/
article/why-we-are-wired-to-connect.

Crabtree, Steve. "In U.S., Depression Rates Higher for
Long-Term Unemployed." Gallup.com. January 8, 2008.
www.gallup.com/poll/171044/depression-rates-higher-
among-long-term-unemployed.aspx.

"Digital Media Literacy: What Is an Echo
Chamber?" GCFGlobal.org, 18 June 2019, edu.gcfglobal.
org/en/digital-media-literacy/what-is-an-echo-chamber/1/.

Goldsmith, Barton. "Having a Purpose Is Paramount
to Beating Depression." psychologytoday.com. May 18,
2018. www.psychologytoday.com/us/blog/emotional-
fitness/201805/having-purpose-is-paramount-beating-
depression.

Gramlich, J. "10 facts about Americans and Facebook."
pewresearchcenter.org. July 31, 2020. www.pewresearch.
org/fact-tank/2019/05/16/facts-about-americans-and-
facebook (accessed November 12, 2020).

Heger, Erin. "7 Benefits of Meditation, and How It Can Affect Your Brain." nsider.com. June 22, 2020. www.insider.com/benefits-of-meditation.

Higgs, Micaela Marini. "How to Deal with Job Search Depression." nytimes.com. May 27, 2019. www.nytimes.com/2019/05/27/smarter-living/how-to-deal-with-job-search-depression.html.

Hughes, Hilary. "Mariah Carey on Being the Top Female Solo Artist of All Time and Loving All Her 'Little Song Babies.'" billboard.com. April 14, 2020. www.billboard.com/articles/columns/pop/8543409/mariah-carey-top-female-solo-artist-interview.

Koskie, Brandi. "Depression: Facts, Statistics, and You." healthline.com. June 3, 2020. www.healthline.com/health/depression/facts-statistics-infographic.

Meyers, Sarah. "25 Self-Made Billionaires and What They Did in Their Twenties." rolustech.com. April 8, 2019. www.rolustech.com/blog/25-billionaires-and-what-they-did-in-their-twenties.

National Institute on Alcohol Abuse and Alcoholism. "Alcohol Use Disorder." U.S. Department of Health and Human Services. www.niaaa.nih.gov/alcohols-effects-health/alcohol-use-disorder.

National Institute on Alcohol Abuse and Alcoholism, U.S. Department of Health and Human Services. "Alcohol Facts and Statistics." www.niaaa.nih.gov/publications/brochures-and-fact-sheets/alcohol-facts-and-statistics (accessed February 18, 2020).

British Broadcasting Corporation. "*New Yorker* Fires Jeffrey Toobin for Exposing Himself on Zoom." BBC.com. November 11,2020. https://www.bbc.com/news/world-us-canada-54912610 (accessed November 12, 2020).

Obama, Barack. "The Long-Shot Candidate." CBS *60 Minutes*. Streamed live on December 28, 2008. YouTube video. www.youtube.com/watch?v=F8MxP9adPO8.

Ritschel, Chelsea. "The Reasons American Adults Find It Hard to Make New Friends." independent.co.uk. May 9, 2019. www.independent.co.uk/life-style/friends-adults-american-how-friendship-difficulty-a8906861.html.

Trust, Gary. "Mariah Carey Becomes First Artist at No. 1 on Billboard Hot 100 in Four Decades, Thanks to 'All I Want for Christmas.'" billboard.com. May 26, 2020. www.billboard.com/articles/business/chart-beat/8547157/mariah-carey-number-one-hot-100-four-decades-all-i-want-for-christmas-is-you.

U.S. News and World Report. "Naming a Street After MLK Is Easier Said Than Done." usnews.com. January 20, 2020. www.usnews.com/news/cities/articles/2020-01-20/for-many-us-towns-and-cities-naming-a-street-after-martin-luther-king-jr-reflects-his-unfinished-work.

Witters, Dan. "Employed Americans in Better Health Than the Unemployed." Gallup.com. July 21,2020. news.gallup.com/poll/155408/Employed-Americans-Better-Health-Unemployed.aspx.

About the Author

BORN ON JANUARY 7, in Dayton, Ohio. Christopher Michael Sumlin was born destined for Greatness. He comes from a tight-knit family, he is the second oldest of four children. Chris has two brothers and a younger sister. He grew up in a Christian household in Columbus, OH. His father was a minister and church was the basis of Chris' young adult life. At age 14, Chris attended a high school called The Charles School at Ohio Dominican University in Columbus. With the love and support of family and mentors, Chris graduated from the school in five years earning both his high school diploma and Associate of Arts degree from Ohio Dominican University.

As a scholar of television in 2015, Chris interned at both FOX Studios and the BET Awards in Los Angeles, California. During his time in Los Angeles, Chris spent a lot of time alone reflecting and studying self help books. His adventures inspired him to write his debut book, *Dealing With This Thing Called Life,* which was released on April 6, 2016. In 2017, Chris graduated from the historic Morehouse College in Atlanta, Georgia, majoring in Cinema, Television & Emerging Media Studies. His time at Morehouse lead him to write his second book, *Dealing With This Thing Called College*, which was released in February of 2018. Both of his books are available on Amazon.

On January 25, 2019, Chris earned his third college degree, a Master's of Science in Television from Boston University.

Today, Chris spends his time writing blogs and speaking to students. It is Chris' plan to use his life experiences to inspire all those he encounters to dream big.

To learn more about Chris Sumlin, visit his website at
www.thechrissumlin.com.